Beating the Odds
Crime, Poverty, and Life in the Inner City

Revised Edition

Robert P. McNamara

CWLA Press • Washington, DC

CWLA Press is an imprint of the Child Welfare League of America. The Child Welfare League of America (CWLA), the nation's oldest and largest membership-based child welfare organization, is committed to engaging all Americans in promoting the well-being of children and protecting every child from harm.

CHILD WELFARE LEAGUE OF AMERICA, INC.
440 First Street, NW, Third Floor, Washington, DC 20001-2085
E-mail: books@cwla.org

CURRENT PRINTING (last digit)
10 9 8 7 6 5 4 3 2 1

Cover design by Luke Johnson

Printed in the United States of America

ISBN # 0–87868-765-3

Library of Congress Cataloging-in-Publication Data
McNamara, Robert P.
    Beating the odds : crime, poverty, and life in the inner city /
Robert P. McNamara. -- Rev. ed.
        p.   cm.
    Includes bibliographical references.
    ISBN 0-87868-765-3
    1. McNamara, Robert P.   2. Urban poor--United States--Biography.
3. Sociologists--United States--Biography.   4. Inner cities--United
States.   5. Poor children--United States.   6. Problem families--
United States.   I. Child Welfare League of America.   II. Title
HV4045.M36   1999   99-20811
362.7'0973--dc21   CIP

Contents

Acknowledgments

To Dan and Mary Ann, who allowed me the time, space, and hope I needed to become the type of person I wanted to be. We may not share the same last name, but there is no one else I would want to call my parents.

To Kristy, my best friend, my wife, and the one person who has taught me more about myself than anyone else. I could never have conceived of this project without your help in healing the old wounds.

And to my three older brothers, for always trying to keep your little brother out of harm's way. You did the best you could, under the circumstances, and I will always be grateful.

Preface

I have spent several years contemplating this project. I am a private person by nature and I have always been skeptical of biographies, since they often seemed to me to be efforts at self-aggrandizement. They are usually written by famous people, those who have had interesting lives, or, more recently, those who want to capture their 15 minutes of fame and huge advances from publishers (e.g., O.J. Simpson and Susan Smith).

I have not led what I can honestly call an "interesting" life, and I certainly have no claim to fame in the media. Thus, when I thought about writing this book, I wondered why I should even be engaging in this type of mental gymnastics. Further, my privacy has always been important to me, so why would I want to write about extremely painful and personal events? To be honest, it has taken me a long time to be able to answer those questions.

As a sociologist and university professor, I think there is something to be learned from this story. It transcends what we may broadly call "human interest," although I am sure some will read it for those reasons. Rather, I feel that many of my experiences relate to some of the most important issues of our time, specifically, racism, prejudice and discrimination, poverty, the declining influence of the family, crime and youth gangs, as well as the importance of role models in resolving some of these problems. I have experienced many of these problems in a rather unique way and hope that I can bring a few interesting insights to the discussion.

On a personal level, some might say that this book opens up a number of deep and painful wounds that are best left alone. In some instances that may be true: the scar tissue is still a little tender. I believe that my willingness to write about these experiences has had a healing effect, however. Instead of looking at this as a painful experience, I feel that I am now able to talk candidly about them. Not that I am completely recovered, since I do not think that will ever happen, but I am at a point in my life where I can deal with them in a relatively objective manner. In short, while there may seem to be a number of academic and objective reasons for writing this book, there are also some rather selfish ones as well. It has shown me that I am on the right track and it has helped me to understand more about the human ability to adapt to adversity.

I cannot take full credit for reaching this level of mental health, however. There are several people that have been of immeasurable help to me. First, there are my parents. I use this term in its truest sense because a parent is a social role, not a biological one. Virtually anyone can create a child—what is much more difficult is to raise one. I feel that Dan and Mary Ann Hartmann have captured the meaning of this distinction. Without them, I know I would never be where I am today. While it is true that some of the credit should be given to me for my work ethic and ambition, I needed the chance to grow. This is something I will come back to in the following pages, but for now, recognize that they have been the catalysts to my success.

Another extremely important part of my success has been my wife Kristy. She has been instrumental in getting me to address some of the most painful emotions/memories, and to help me repair my relationships with several family members. Without getting too philosophical, she has allowed me to see another side of who I am and to allow that side to grow. Also of importance are two of my brothers, Brad and Mark, who have been supportive of me in many different ways, especially in graduate school. In a different way, my brother Daryl has also helped. Our dramatic contrasts have always been a source of wonder and motivation to me and his path in life also serves as a good example of one of the most perplexing riddles of modern times: what influences people's behavior—innate drives or environmental factors? Daryl and I came from the same place with many of the same problems, yet today his whereabouts are unknown and he leaves in his wake a storied and violent past.

On a professional level, Dennis Kenney, Albert J. Reiss, Kai Erikson, Bill Kornblum, and Eugene Fappiano have played important roles in my professional growth. Of this distinguished group, Dennis has been perhaps the most influential. I have known him for approximately 11 years and he has always been there for advice, opportunities, and an encouraging comment or two. While I know he does not prefer the use of the term mentor, in its truest form, it really does best describe our relationship. He has been a good friend and colleague.

There are other people who helped make this project a reality. Maria Tempenis deserves credit for tracking down some of the more obscure pieces of information for this project. She is one of the most talented students I have ever known, and I have come to admire her diligence and work ethic. While still an undergraduate, for those who look for talented students to see how they mature and grow intellectually, she possesses that rare gift of talent and motivation. Thanks also goes to John Fuller of the University of West Georgia, Lloyd Benson, Nelly Hecker, John Hoppey, Lesley Quast, Paul Rasmussen, Steve Richardson, Shirley Ritter, and Stephanie Shute, of Furman University, as well as Lieutenant William White of the New Haven Police Department. A special thanks goes to Nina Anthony, who has been of immeasurable help to me in many different ways and has been a wonderful addition to the sociology department at Furman.

There are also a few people who I would like to thank for not believing in me or my abilities. These people know who they are and I hope they have not done to others what they have done to me. I call special attention to the teachers who said I would never amount to anything. You may actually find yourself in a position to read this account and I would urge you to examine the sociological literature on the labeling perspective, especially the concept of the self-fulfilling prophecy. I would also encourage you to think carefully about how you treat your students. In some cases, the damage you do is irreversible. My experiences are daily reminders that students are extremely sensitive about their abilities and need frequent reassurance. With the right approach and sufficient attention, they can flourish. Unfortunately, the inverse is also true and this is something I always try to remember in my interactions with them.

1

The Blue Collar Scholar: Life in the Ivy League

One day I am lecturing on the issues of race and poverty as it relates to education in my course on social problems. In this discussion one student comments:

> But I don't understand, Dr. McNamara. People like you and me are having more and more problems getting a good education and we have the SAT scores and qualifications to get into the best schools. As you mentioned, people from poor backgrounds have trouble getting even a basic education, let alone one that qualifies them go to the best colleges. So if they can't compete, why should we give them spots in the best schools when more qualified students aren't able to get in? I mean how would you feel if some kid from a poor neighborhood was given your spot at Yale? Would you feel differently about things like poverty, affirmative action, and racism?

To be honest, I was not expecting such a dramatic comment. I smiled, thought a moment, and then responded, "What if I told you that I *was* one of those types of people. What if I told you that I went to public schools in urban areas for most of my life and I never even took my SATs?"

"I'd say you were playing the devil's advocate again," the student said.

"Let me tell you a quick story," I began.

Later that same day, I attempted to explain the labeling perspective to students in my deviance course. In the course of that discussion, several students were adamant concerning the treatment of deviance. They argued that if a person committed a deviant or criminal act, they should forever be outcast from society. When I asked these students if they thought that the offender, such as a former gang member who engaged in a variety of deviant/criminal acts, could ever make a positive contribution to society, they firmly stated that it was impossible. A bit exasperated, I asked them, "What if I told you I was a former gang member who engaged in a variety of criminal acts?" None of the students believed me. I proceeded to create a simple ledger on the board of the positive things people on campus knew about me (my qualifications, publications, teaching awards, etc.) and then included some previously unknown bits of information on the other side of the ledger. A few stated that I could not have come from "that kind of background." Others contended that I was being overly sensational. After pressing them a bit further about the possibility of this scenario occurring, one student commented that he would have a higher level of respect for a person who was able to overcome the negative effects of these experiences and still achieve a measure of success.

As exasperating as they were, having these conversations with my students was the first time I ever thought about this project or even of writing about the events that led up to my experiences at Yale. It caused me to think that I had something important to contribute to the discussions on these topics, and, perhaps more important, that my students could better understand a perspective on these issues that is different from the one to which they have traditionally been exposed. These two classes were my first group of Furman University students and, for many reasons, I owe them an important debt of thanks. For now, allow me to take a step back and describe the circumstances that led me to the Ivy League.

Getting into Yale

To be honest, I never even gave much thought to college, at least not initially. I was not what one might call a model student. In fact, I came close to being expelled from high school and almost did not graduate because of a restrictive attendance policy. As I will describe in greater detail in another chapter, by the time I reached high school I was suffering from a lot of emotional baggage, as well as a healthy dose of culture shock. I was a street kid in a high school full of affluence and elitism. Add to the fact that I despised arrogance in people and had the verbal and physical skills (and inclination) to make my feelings known, and the results were rather predictable.

My goal was to be a police officer. I read the book *Serpico* by Peter Maas when I was in junior high school and from that point on, I knew what wanted to do. While some of the kids in my high school class talked about going to college, I thought that I would simply sign up for the police academy. The fact that I knew nothing about the selection process made little difference. I did not think I would have the chance to go to college, even if I wanted to.

For two of the three years I spent at Chichester High School, I worked full-time as a cook at a local restaurant. Given that my shift often did not end until two or three in the morning, especially on Fridays, getting up before eight o'clock on a Saturday morning to take the SATs did not seem like a good idea to me. So while my friends and acquaintances crammed, I kept a stack of uncashed paychecks in my sock drawer.

After a period of time, which included a bus trip to California to follow a girl, and a return stint at home, I went to work making sandwiches for a fast food chain. It was a small company, and the two partners owned six franchised stores. I quickly became their regional manager, responsible for three of the six stores. It was during this time that I became fascinated with the law. I had a host of regulations to follow, a dozen inspectors of various sorts to deal with, and a variety of state, federal, and local ordinances with which to comply. I had always been interested in crime, so I started taking classes part-time at a local community college. By then I was tired of the 100-hour work weeks and the daily stress of dealing with approximately 25 employees, most of whom were college students who worked part-time and had little attachment to the job. I had decided to become a lawyer, a prosecutor. The flame was lit and I decided to quit my job and attend school full-time.

I read everything I could get my hands on. I was fascinated by the Supreme Court, reading as many biographies on the Justices as I could find. I read *The Court Years* [1981] and *Go East Young Man* [1974] by William O. Douglas; G. Edward White's [1982] book entitled *Earl Warren*; Bob Woodward and Scott Armstrong's [1979] *The Brethren*; Wallace Mendelson's [1961] *Justice Black and Frankfurter: Conflict in the Court*; Stephen Strickland's 1967 *Hugo Black and the Supreme Court*; and Everette Dennis, Donald Gillmor and David Grey's [1978] *Justice Hugo Black and the First Amendment*, to name a few. Justice Black was perhaps the most interesting Justice about which to read, although I think Justice Douglas impressed me the most intellectually.

I also had the utmost respect for Thurgood Marshall. I had read Richard Kluger's [1975] *Simple Justice*, which captures the events surrounding the *Brown v. Board of Education* case and was moved by Marshall's courage and conviction. In fact, I was so impressed that I wrote to him and described the impact this book, and his work, had on me. It was the first time I had ever done anything like that, but it was a powerful piece of work and I wanted him to know how I felt.

Above all, I was interested in the way the Court shaped social policy, especially as it related to the police. I was particularly interested in the Warren Court and its many landmark decisions concerning the rights of the individual, as well as the restrictions placed on police procedure. As I describe elsewhere in lectures and presentations, I have since come to believe that these restrictions are part of a cyclical effect of our society's need to exert control over the justice process.

While trying to read as much as I could on the Court, as well as the police, I finished the requirements for the Associate's Degree a year later and transferred to a state university for my undergraduate degree. I looked upon my undergraduate days as a rite of passage by which I could gain entry into law school. Everything was focused toward that goal. I used to tell people that the only reason I earned a Bachelor's degree was because, like the LSAT, it was a requirement for admission. Parenthetically, I even looked for some law schools that did not require a four-year degree.

Western Connecticut State University (WestConn) seemed tailor-made for me: it was a degree in criminal justice (although they called it Justice and Law Administration), it had a strong program for students who wanted to pursue a legal career, it was by far the cheapest of all the four-year schools in the state, and it was relatively small in terms of its overall population. The only problem was that it was located about 60 miles from where I lived at the time.

For two years I made the commute, often five days per week. I made the best of it because I was determined to have an impressive academic record so that I could choose whatever law school I wanted. I think it is ironic that it was at this school that I met the person who would have the most influence on my professional life: Dennis Kenney. After working for him I came to realize that law school was not really what I wanted to do at all. In fact, I owe him an eternal debt of gratitude for exposing me to a field of study that I have made into a career.

Initially however, he and I did not exactly hit it off. In fact, he was responsible for many hours of frustration and anxiety. We laugh about it now, but I actually expanded my vocabulary of profanity in describing his courses. I thought him to be overly demanding and a major pain in the neck. When I looked back on each semester, however, I found it was in his courses that I gained the most knowledge and insight. I worked harder for my grade than at any other time, but I was also rewarded for my efforts.

It was also during this time that I decided I was going to reward the faculty member who had, in my opinion, done the most outstanding job in terms of teaching for that year. I had started this during my last semester at Mattatuck Community College. I gave the Chair of the Criminal Justice program a gift, because I felt he had given me the foundation I needed from which to continue my studies. After my first year with Dennis, where I took courses with him during both semesters, I felt he had done the same thing.

I know this may sound obsequious and underhanded, but I was not looking for a better grade. I had already earned the highest marks in the class, so I felt it would not be perceived as a bribe. I merely wanted to let him know that I really appreciated what he had done for me. (Upon reflection, this is something I have always done to people who have helped me. I am genuinely surprised when people give me things or do things for me. And when that occurs, I have this need to repay them in some way. In this instance, I was doing the same thing.)

With each passing lecture, I knew I had made the right decision to focus on issues relating to criminal justice rather than on legal research. Dennis taught me how to think like a scholar, to see the unintended consequences of events and phenomena, and I could not get enough of it. During my senior year I had the opportunity to become his research assistant, the first in the department. It was during this time that I really began to question whether or not law school was where I wanted to spend my time. This went beyond the typical case of apprehension that many undergraduates go through in their senior year. For me, I had worked diligently toward a single goal: to get into law school. Now that goal was in question. I found the research on crime more fascinating than anything else I had done. For six agonizing weeks I debated whether to apply to graduate school or law school. Some programs offered dual degree programs, but I thought that would not suffice for me. I had to make a decision and I knew hedging my bet like that would only prolong the inevitable.

The problem was that there were no graduate programs that offered a Ph.D. in criminal justice. I decided to try Rutgers University, largely because of its reputation and because it was relatively close, an hour's drive from WestConn. The graduate school is located in Newark, New Jersey. To most people, a three-hour commute does not fall into the category of "nearby." I thought it was worth a try, but soon realized that the demands of the program, as well as the cumulative effect of driving, especially in New Jersey, where aggressiveness does not begin to describe commuters' approach to driving, simply wore me out.

I was stuck. Where was I going to go to get at least a Master's Degree in Criminal Justice, and, ultimately a Ph.D.? One day I was looking through Rutger's graduate catalog and saw the names of faculty members and their academic credentials. I noticed that most were either in sociology or psychology. Suddenly an idea began to emerge. I would become a sociologist who studied crime. After all, if some of the greatest minds in criminal justice had sociological backgrounds, I could get similar training. As an additional benefit, I had read many sociological accounts of crime and criminals and became interested in the Chicago School and qualitative research.

With this in mind, I decided that I needed some background in sociology, preferably a Master's Degree, before I pursued the Ph.D. I found a school near my home that not only offered a Master's Degree in Sociology, but also had an emphasis in Criminal Justice. An added bonus was that it was relatively inexpensive. As a part of the University of Connecticut system, Southern Connecticut State University does not have the reputation of Rutgers or Yale, but it gave me the chance to try my hand at being a sociologist. Still smarting from what I perceived as my failure at Rutgers, I had something to prove to myself. I felt that I would give Southern my best effort and if that did not work, I would pursue another career.

In my first two courses at Southern, I met Eugene Fappiano, one of the truly great people of our society. A man of vast knowledge and a dedication to his students, Gene inspired me to become better. He encouraged me, would spend hours talking to me about topics of interest, and would mention text after text that would be helpful. I tracked down those books, read them, and came back for more. Before I knew it, I was turning into a sociologist.

It did not take long to complete the requirements for the degree. Then the problems of finding a school with a Ph.D. program began. I learned that one of the most respected scholars in the field, Albert Cohen, was a professor at the University of Connecticut. The main campus is located in Storrs, Connecticut, about an hour's drive from where I was living at the time. Moreover, I would not have to attend classes five days per week. I also applied to the John Jay School of Criminal Justice in New York City. This program offered the types of courses that I really wanted to immerse myself in. It was two hours away, but by then my financial situation had improved and I thought that I could take the train into the city.

Finally, on a whim, I applied to Yale. I learned that one of the leading scholars in criminal justice, Albert J. Reiss Jr., was a professor there (he too is a sociologist by training). I had read one of his books in high school and thought it was worth the gamble. To my surprise, Yale was the first school to accept me. John Jay was uncertain about my credentials and wanted to interview me, and to this day the University of Connecticut still has not made a decision on my candidacy. For a while I kept calling to see what had happened, but one of the secretaries kept insisting that the Admission's Office had not quite made up their minds about me. At one point the secretary used words to the effect that officials simply were uncertain if I would make a valuable contribution to their program. After completing the requirements for the Ph.D. at Yale, a friend of mine suggested that I send them a copy of my diploma and ask them if it would help them in making their decision about letting me into their program. Who knows? Maybe it would help.

The odd thing about this situation was that I did not want to go to Yale. I thought I would spend far too much time in courses that meant little to me. I wanted courses on crime, deviance, field research, and criminal justice. While Yale advertised courses like that, I found that few were offered. I was, however, able to take courses in deviance and field research with Albert Reiss, as well as a seminar in qualitative methods with Kai Erikson, and these were perhaps the most interesting of all the courses I selected. Initially, though, I had some concerns about how I would fit in at a place like Yale.

Unknowingly, one of my brothers helped me make this decision. When I called him about being accepted and, more importantly, that I had second thoughts about going, he wondered aloud if I was mentally ill. In his own way, he told me that I was crazy to turn down an opportunity like this one. His words of advice caused me to reconsider my decision. After all, I could hang out with Reiss and use the Yale name when I finished to obtain the best possible job. Besides, I was to receive a scholarship that paid my tuition... how could I lose? As it turned out, I benefited greatly from this decision. I met some interesting people, largely because of my affiliation with Yale (and Reiss and Erikson), and I believe it has allowed me to obtain the kind of academic position I desired. Some of my colleagues at Yale thought I was shortchanging my degree, because I wanted to teach at a small school where I could get to know my students. "Why go to one of the most prestigious research universities in the world if you are only going to a small school?" they would say. To me, the degree made me marketable at a small school: it did not shortchange me. And this was exactly why I chose Yale in the first place.

These types of situations only confirmed what I had initially suspected: I was not a "Yalie," nor would I ever really fit in there. This is not to say that the environment was hostile or that I did not make friends while I was there. Rather, it meant that I had more in common with the secretaries and the housekeeping staff than I did with many of my colleagues and professors.

Life at Yale

The five years I spent at Yale were well worth the time. While many of my fellow graduate students have taken longer to finish, and thereby extended the protective cocoonlike atmosphere, I felt that graduate school had to be viewed as a means to an end rather than an end unto itself. In short, I was in a hurry to get on with my life as a scholar and although I will look back on my time spent there with positive thoughts, it was clear to me that I could not allow myself to fall into that trap.

Most of my colleagues had usually spent time in prep schools or private high schools, and many had earned their undergraduate degrees from other ivy league institutions. At the least, virtually all of them came from what one might call a privileged background. This did not exactly allow me to immerse myself into the student culture easily. While I got along fine with most of them, I found that since I did not explore Pierre Bourdieu or Jurgen Habermas in my free time, nor did I have the time to meet and discuss the finer points of their theories, I found I had little in common with them. I have never had the opportunities that allowed that type of lifestyle. I understand the finer points, and when needed, read the works of the various scholars. The difference, however, was that I had little time (or inclination) to do so when I had a free moment.

This is not meant to be a criticism of my colleagues' life chances, it simply means that I always felt a bit on the outside of the student culture. This was okay with me, since I did not have time to worry about it. After all, I had work to do.

During my tenure as a graduate student, I worked several part-time jobs to make ends meet. I taught courses at a nearby state university, tended bar part-time for a local catering company, and, early in my graduate program, I worked as a security guard at a hospital and the Yale Art Museum. Later, I left the job at the hospital to work as a consultant on a research project under the auspices of the Centers for Disease Control and Prevention. Juggling a full-time course load and chasing income was a formidable task, to say the least. It forced me to be organized, and I believe this helped me later when I worked on my dissertation. It was also good training after graduate school, where I am able to manage several projects simultaneously, create new courses, and spend a lot of time with my students outside of class.

Perhaps the most important thing that the university gave me is the opportunity to meet my wife. We entered graduate school together and quickly became friends. It is not uncommon for new students to pair off and work together when they arrive in graduate school. In some places, team work becomes the norm (e.g., law school) since it is impossible to complete all the work alone. Kristy and I became friends not only out of the need to survive, but because we had a lot of commonality in terms of our backgrounds.

One of my fondest memories of my time spent with Kristy occurred shortly after we began classes our first year. She spent her undergraduate days in the rolling hills of Vermont and was suddenly thrust into an urban environment, with all the problems and risks that come with it. Since she lived a couple of blocks away from campus, near the Ingalls Rink, and because the weather was still favorable, coupled with the parking problems endemic to New Haven, she decided to walk to and from classes each day. When I discovered this, and became concerned about her safety, I offered to give her a ride home each day. At first she accepted but then her stubbornness took over. Actually, she is quite independent, and I suspect the reason for her refusal had more to do with asserting that quality than anything else. To be fair, I admired that characteristic but given that this was a dangerous neighborhood, one that I was familiar with, I began to insist. While she kept refusing, I finally convinced her that it was better to accept the ride than for me to drive alongside her on the street as she walked on the sidewalk back to her apartment. I am grateful that she did not challenge me on this, because the street was lined with parked cars on one side and this left barely enough room for one vehicle. Had a car turned on to the street, I would have had to leave her and circle the block.

One event took place that perhaps best captures the difficulties I had fitting into a place like Yale. In 1989, graduate students, who were tired of being exploited as teaching assistants, decided to form a union. They called it GESO, which stood for Graduate Employee and Student Organization. Essentially, students were arguing that they were overworked for the amount of money they received. They also argued that the amount of money teaching assistants were given at Yale was considerably lower than what their counterparts at Harvard, Columbia, and Princeton were receiving. This had been a long-standing problem between the graduate students and the university. According to GESO records, the genesis for the union began in 1972, with philosophy grad students who were working as teaching assistants (TA). The students were unhappy with the amount they were paid, as well as the number of hours they worked. The university responded by claiming that the students were paid honorariums and not salaries, and, as such, were not university employees [GESO 1995].

The problem continued, even though a teaching assistant organization was established in April 1972 to improve salaries, limit workloads, and to require the university full disclosure of their budget. Fourteen years later, the contentions on the part of the graduate students remained and in the spring of 1987, the teaching assistants formed TA Solidarity (TAS), which was a modern version of the 1972 organization. In response to the pressure exerted by TAS concerning low salaries and longer hours, the university continued to address the needs of their graduate students in a noncommittal manner. Throughout this period, and until this writing, the university and GESO have been at odds with regard to their status on campus. GESO even organized a three-day strike in 1992, with the support of other university unions, to protest what they argued were unfair labor practices [GESO 1995]. As the battle continued, with the university reneging on promises related to workload and increased wages, Yale was in the midst of one of the most controversial proposals in its history: the termination of several departments, including sociology, due to what had been called a fiscal crisis.

Yale had contended that they were so financially strapped that they would need to close certain departments and, where possible, assign faculty to other disciplines. This sent the campus, and the sociology department, into a swirl of anger and protest. Faculty, students, staff, and many others not affiliated with the university questioned whether or not Yale was being honest in their assertions concerning financial matters. The suspicions were compounded when the university refused to allow anyone to examine their financial records. It was indeed a time of tension around New Haven.

One of my friends was active in the student movement and asked if I would participate in the strike. I had many problems with GESO's platform and had great difficulty identifying and rallying behind the cause. I was being paid approximately $3,000 to grade exams and papers and to lead discussions with students once a week on the readings for that topic. As an acting instructor, I was paid more than $4,000 to simply give a lecture, to hold office hours, and to provide direction to my teaching assistants. Most of the classes averaged around 30 to 35 students, although there were some that were quite large. Upper level courses were usually smaller, usually around 25. To warrant a teaching assistant, however, the class size had to be in increments of 50: for every 50 students, the instructor received one teaching assistant.

As an adjunct faculty member at Southern Connecticut State University, a local university, I was responsible for lecturing and grading, as well as all administrative tasks. Moreover, my courses typically averaged 42 students. For all this I received, after 30 credits of teaching experience, $2,020. Additionally, this was one of the more lucrative university positions in the area. At a small liberal arts college in another part of town, the salary for adjunct work was a bit more than $1,000. Thus, the argument made by many of the graduate students about being oppressed and exploited was not reflective of the actual market conditions. In other words, they were talking to the wrong guy about how "bad it is out there." I tried to explain this to my friend, to no avail. Did I not see the bigger issue, he asked me? Could I not identify with my colleagues and show some social solidarity, even if it were only a symbolic form?

Quite honestly, the answer was no. I could not identify with people who were complaining when they received a lot more money than I did for doing a lot less work. This was how it was for me at Yale. Things that interested my colleagues were of little interest to me or I had no time to play. Moreover, I had a difficult time seeing the relevance of issues that were considered important to many of them. To say I never really fit into the student subculture at Yale is, I think, an accurate statement. Fortunately, I was able to make a few lasting friends during my time. These people remain important to me and I try to keep in touch with them.

The irony of the entire situation at Yale was that they seemed reluctant to take a chance on me. There was a cohort of 11 that entered the program in 1988, and virtually everyone was on some sort of financial aid or stipend. In the beginning, Yale offered me one-half tuition waiver, which was increased to a full waiver just before I arrived on campus. Kristy and I were both given the same award and, while it may be coincidence, our increase in aid came at about the same time that a student who had a full waiver decided not to attend that year. While it may be only speculation on our part, we believe this was the only reason our financial awards were increased. So where is the irony? As of 1995, of the 11 of us that began the program, only four have finished, the latter two in this past year. Moreover, Kristy and I were able to finish in five years. So much for the wisdom of the scholarship decision.

Again, I do not mean to berate Yale, the department, or any of my colleagues. In fact, I feel that I was given a tremendous opportunity to succeed, and I took advantage of that. What I am saying is that by simply relying on quantitative data/criteria, mistakes will be made. To borrow from the great Max Weber, one of the giants of sociology, we have become too rational in our decisionmaking and social interactions. Another way of saying this is that we spend too much time looking at the person's qualifications and not enough at the total package. I must admit, however, that this is how the "game" is played. In fact, it is the reason why I chose to attend Yale. There are some extremely talented people at less prestigious universities, however, and there are some decidedly average people who attend Yale. Unfortunately, we tend to base most of our understanding of a person based on a few cues.

Life After Yale

While finishing my dissertation, my wife and I entered the job market. This was not exactly an enjoyable experience. I had always thought that I wanted to remain in the New England area. Kristy and I had family in Connecticut and Massachusetts, and I thought that with a Ph.D. from a place like Yale and a location like the Northeast, with a host of colleges and universities, we would not have any problem finding jobs. Additionally, the projected trends indicated that there would be a large number of professors retiring around the time that we would be entering the market.

Despite the projected boom, the academic market continues to be a depressed one. The calculations did not take into account a change in the economy. Thus, while there may have been positions available at some schools due to retirement, fiscal austerity prevented them from being filled. As a result, Kristy and I had a bit of trouble finding jobs. While there were some offers, most were for one position or they were in different parts of the country. In other cases, the demands placed on the faculty were simply unreasonable. To require a heavy teaching load and expect an active research agenda, we thought, was simply unacceptable. It is difficult to manage both of those things, even when the university is clear about its mission. In some cases, the schools called themselves teaching institutions, but it was clear they wanted their faculty to bring in grant money. No thanks. We both wanted a university that cared about its students, that allowed us to become active in campus life, and did not put us in a "publish or perish" situation. We wanted to be active, but on our own terms.

Kristy interviewed at Furman University and became quite enamored with the collegial atmosphere. I wanted to spend some time with first generation students, with whom I tend to identify. I was appointed to the Department of Sociology/Anthropology as an Assistant Professor of Sociology and Criminal Justice at West Georgia College, which is located in Carrollton, Georgia. This required a three-hour commute and an intense and wearing schedule. Here we were, possessing Ph.D.s from Yale, and we were having trouble finding jobs in the same state.

Fortunately, West Georgia allowed me the benefit of a three-day-per-week schedule. I would make the commute on Tuesday morning, teach classes, hold office hours, write lectures, etc., and leave on Thursday evening. During this time, both Kristy and I continued to apply for jobs in each other's area in the hope of finding a position at the same school. A few months after Kristy started, a position became available in her department. Several months later, I became the newest sociologist at Furman University. With the support of the faculty, I have had the opportunity to get to know my students, to work with them, and to provide a number of opportunities for them to grow intellectually. Were it not for Furman's strong commitment to teaching and providing a liberal arts education within a Christian atmosphere, I would not have been able to work toward achieving many of my goals as an educator.

Furman University is a small independent liberal arts college in Greenville, South Carolina. It has about 2,500 undergraduates, most of whom are from the Southeastern region of the United States. It is an institution strongly committed to teaching and to providing a solid academic foundation for its students. For example, many of the faculty talk about the "Furman family" as a way of describing the relationships the university has with its students, faculty, and staff. While it may sound like a publicity statement, I have found that this is one of the most collegial places I have ever known. Students want to come back, faculty work in the spirit of cooperation, and there does seem to be a strong sense of community on campus. Evidence of this is found in the many members of the faculty and a large percentage of students who participate in volunteer activities. Additionally, in the spirit of education, there are a host of opportunities for faculty and students to engage in various types of research. This may sound like a recruitment speech, but it is not. Furman has its problems like every other institution, but overall, it is a wonderful place to work and I am grateful to have had the chance to join the faculty.

Thus, while it seems that life has turned out great for me, I cannot forget where I came from. For a good portion of my life, things were not always so wonderful. There are others who had it worse than I did, but in reality, I was a lot like many other kids in our society who are trapped by life in the inner city. In fact, as I will argue in subsequent pages, were it not for a few important opportunities, I could easily have ended up a drug addict, in prison, or dead, like many of the people I grew up with in the old neighborhood. It is with this in mind that I attempt to describe the events and circumstances that brought me to my current position. In some cases, such as where the events are still too painful to discuss or are not relevant to the discussion, I have omitted them.

A word on methodology. It is important to recognize that this is not simply an account based on my own memory or perception of events. Wherever possible, I have attempted to verify the chronological events by gaining access to my case file from the Department of Child and Families (DCF) for the State of Connecticut, school records, police reports, personal diaries, and interviews with individuals who could offer some assessment of the situation.

Still, as Berger and Luckman [1967] describe in their seminal piece, *The Social Construction of Reality*, it must be remembered that what I am about to describe is my *recollection* of events. In some cases, such as the later years, it is done through the lens of an adult, and in others, it is from the perspective of an 8-year-old. This does not mean the account is an inaccurate one, it simply means that my memory of events might be different from others simply because, as Berger and Luckman describe, *their* version of reality was constructed somewhat differently. That is not to say that their version is more accurate than mine, rather it means we witnessed events from different vantage points.

Additionally, I have also included a discussion of the relevant literature on the various topics covered in this book. This does not necessarily mean that the literature validates the account, rather it is a way of framing my recollection of events and to offer an assessment of the situation. In no way do I mean to suggest that the literature serves as a verification of the accuracy of my observations. It is simply my way of placing what I believe happened in a sociological context and to show that this is not, at first glance, as exceptional as one might think.

Providing this context has additional advantages. For example, if the reader is interested in learning about the poverty debate from an empirical point of view, it will be provided. On the other hand, if he or she would like to have some context in which this discussion is given, such as a first-person account of how the abstract theory relates to reality, or is simply interested in the "story" for its dramatic value, he or she will find something useful here as well. I think this blend of the sociological literature combined with a biographical account is unusual, but it is also the book's strongest point.

Chapter 2 provides a profile of life in the city of New Haven during the 1960s and 1970s, as well as background on my family situation. Due to concerns about legal liability, when necessary, I will be altering the names of the participants and/or disguising the environments in such a way that it protects the identities of those involved. This includes not only my family, but friends, associates, and anyone else who may be harmed by the discussion.

Chapter 3 focuses on the breakup of my family, the various families with whom I lived, as well as issues surrounding single parent families. Chapter 4 describes my involvement with crime and gangs, while Chapter 5 raises the issue of race, class, prejudice, and discrimination. In other words, it describes my life as a "minority." This is a sensitive issue to many, including myself, and I will attempt to place the events in their historical and social contexts.

Chapter 6 includes a discussion of governmental involvement in the breakup of families, specifically foster care. Chapter 7 describes the problems I encountered with the upper social class, as well as the labeling perspective of deviance. This is also the point in the story where I met my parents and the impact they had on me as role models. In Chapter 8, I spend time elaborating on the issues raised in Chapter 7, as well as showing how the solutions we have created to rectify many of society's social problems have failed to achieve their intended effect. If anything, we continue to repeat the same mistakes again and again.

In sum, I have written this book in an effort to help others understand the nature of the problems "minorities" and the disadvantaged face in our society. I have also written it with the hope that if other young people find themselves in a similar situation, they will not lose hope or belief in themselves.

Finally, I have written this book to encourage others who have "made it" into helping those who have not. As I tell my students, with the privilege of going first and achieving success comes the responsibility of helping those who are behind them. With any luck, this book will have prompted someone to pause and contemplate the role they are playing in other people's lives. While little can be done to rectify the problems I endured, there is a great deal that can be done to ensure that others do not have to encounter the same fate. If there is anything positive to come from this book, I would like it to be the recognition that it does not have to happen again.

References

Berger, P. L., & Luckman, T. (1967). *The social construction of reality: A treatise in the sociology of knowledge*. New York: Anchor.

Dennis, E. E., Gillmor, D. M., & Gray, D. L. (1978). *Justice Hugo Black and the First Amendment*. Ames, IA: Iowa State University Press.

Douglas, W. O. (1981). *The Court years: The autobiography of William O. Douglas.* New York: Vintage Books.

Douglas, W. O. (1974). *The autobiography of William O. Douglas: The early years. Go east young man.* New York: Dell.

Graduate Employee and Student Organization [GESO]. (1995). *History of relations between graduate students and the Yale administration.* New Haven, CT: Author.

Kluger, R. (1975). *Simple justice.* New York: Vintage.

Maas, P. (1973). *Serpico.* New York: Viking.

Mendelson, W. (1961). *Justices Black and Frankfurter: Conflict in the Court.* Chicago: University of Chicago Press.

Strickland, S. (Ed.). (1967). *Hugo Black and the Supreme Court.* New York: Bobbs Merrill.

White. G. E. (1982). *Earl Warren: A public life.* New York: Oxford University Press.

Woodward, B., & Armstrong, S. (1979). *The brethren.* New York: Simon and Schuster.

2

The Early Years in New Haven

In the 1960s, the city of New Haven, Connecticut, was a city in transition. It was relatively small by most standards, with a population of approximately 152,000 people, according to the 1960 Census [U.S. Department of Commerce 1960]. Of these, 129,383 or 85% were white, while 22,113 or 14% were African Americans. According to the 1970 Census, the population decreased by 15% (137,707 people), with 72% or 99,986 white, and the African American population almost doubled from the previous decade to 26% or 36,158 [U.S. Department of Commerce 1970].

As with most cities during these turbulent times, New Haven also experienced a number of social problems, such as crime, poverty, racism, and housing. This was also the era of Richard C. Lee, the mayor of the city who was responsible for much of its redevelopment from the late 1950s through the 1970s. During this period, New Haven's physical and social infrastructure had begun to deteriorate, and Lee's formidable mission was to restore the city physically, economically, and culturally.

With help from an infusion of federal funds, spurred on by the Kennedy Administration's desire to do things for and with cities, Lee was able to make great strides in New Haven's development. In fact, many urban planners and other experts referred to New Haven as a "model city" (see Powledge [1970]). For example, in 1959 Wooster Square was known as "Little Naples" and a generation of neglect had turned the area into an industrial slum. This area, a 235-acre plot not far from the center of the city, was first settled by affluent WASPs when New Haven was a commercial sailing port. By 1850, some people referred to it as New Haven's most fashionable neighborhood. But as time went on, the harbor decreased in importance and the city became an industrial center, with immigrants soon arriving. During this period, the WASPs moved out to make way for the Italians. By 1900, the Italians made up almost a quarter of the Wooster Square population, and by the end of the 1960s, they made up about 80% of the 7,000 neighborhood residents [Powledge 1970].

In terms of redevelopment, until 1954, legislation required that land be cleared of buildings to qualify for assistance. However, the Housing Act of that year was amended to allow funding for projects that included the rehabilitation of existing buildings. New Haven became the first city to utilize this provision and the Wooster Square community was designed so that a minimum of buildings would be razed. This resulted in the rehabilitation of many homes and businesses, as well as the construction of the Wooster Square Industrial Park, which brought more than $11 million in private investments to the area [Doomhoff 1978].

The following year, the city began to restore a predominantly African American ghetto: the Dixwell neighborhood, just north of Yale University. Like the Wooster Square project, this plan involved a minimal amount of razing and active participation on the part of the citizens. At about the same time, the city was creating the area known as Long Wharf. By the end of the 1960s, several large manufacturing companies built plants on this strip of land, including the Armstrong Rubber Company [Doomhoff 1978].

In sum, in 1960, $30 million in public and private construction projects had been started. Also in that year, 500 families were relocated and 379 slum buildings were demolished [Talbot 1967]. Many old buildings that could not be saved were being torn down all over the city; homeowners and landlords were being persuaded to rehabilitate their properties; the harbor was becoming something of which to be proud; and the downtown area was also becoming an attractive place to shop. It was an age of optimism. After many years of steady decline, people began to believe that there was hope for New Haven.

The city was not without its problems, however, and the residents of the Hill section of the city, the largest and perhaps poorest of the inner-city neighborhoods, were not as excited or enthusiastic as their more affluent neighbors. Historically a community of Italian working-class families, according to the 1960 Census, the Hill neighborhood was overwhelmingly white (86%), but by 1962 it seemed to be attracting more African American and Hispanic families. This trend included many young African American and Puerto Rican families of childbearing age, with most whites, except the elderly, departing for other neighborhoods.

By 1966, the population in the Hill was approximately 23,000. Of those, about 50% were white, approximately 43% were African American and about 7% were of Hispanic origin [Powledge 1970]. With minor exceptions, the white population in the inner city was composed of the elderly and the childless. The overwhelming majority of the inner city population increase was in the African American and Puerto Rican communities.

The redevelopment efforts had little immediate meaning to people who lived in these neighborhoods. To them, New Haven was not a model city at all. They still had to contend with the problems they had before, the only difference was that the federal government was pouring money into other areas of the city. Riots in 1967 were evidence of the sense of frustration felt by many residents, as well as a lack of belief in any substantial social change.

The Riots

What some residents called a disturbance because it left few injured and had resulted in little property damage, was nevertheless a riot. On Saturday evening August 19, 1967 a Puerto Rican man was shot by a white merchant in the Hill. It was alleged that the Puerto Rican had threatened the white man with a knife and the proprietor shot him, resulting in a minor injury. The Puerto Rican was later charged with aggravated assault and the white man was charged with assault with intent to kill. When news of a racially based incident occurred, violence spread from the Hill to three other poor neighborhoods: Fair Haven, Dixwell, and Newhallville.

Mayor Lee declared a state of emergency, complete with a curfew for all city residents, which lasted for five days.

Later on there was some looting in Wooster Square and even the predominantly white Westville section of the city. Many people were arrested, both African American and white, either for vandalism, looting, or, more commonly, violating the imposed curfew.

It was also during this time that the infamous Black Panther Party came to town. There were many rumors circulating through New Haven about the Party's agenda and the impact they might have on the social climate of the city. These rumors may have had some basis in fact because the National Guard was summoned in an effort to maintain order. The trial of Bobby Seale, one of the founders of the Party, was widely publicized, and flyers with phrases such as "People's Rally to Free Black Panthers" and "Free Bobby Seale" were stapled to trees, telephone poles, and boarded-up windows all around the city.

According to contemporary standards, the riot in New Haven was not especially destructive. The National Advisory Commission on Civil Disorders, established by President Johnson in 1967 to examine the summer violence, examined more than 150 cities reporting racial disorders. It rated the disturbances on a scale of "major," "serious," and "minor." The commission chose New Haven as one of 23 cities for its survey and found New Haven's riot to be "serious." According to the commission, the violence in New Haven started with people throwing rocks and bottles at passing vehicles in the Hill section and was followed by looting, then fires, with the violence gradually tapering off after that.

Thus, while some called New Haven a model city, and there was an air of optimism swirling around the city in the mid- to late-1960s, many of the problems of education, poverty, crime, and white flight remained a fixed feature of the landscape. It was in this environment that I was growing up.

The Early Years

I was born in November 1960, on Frank Street in the Hill section of New Haven, the youngest of four boys. We lived in a small two-family home, which was owned by my maternal grandfather, who lived upstairs. My grandfather was one of the first people to have an impact on me. He was from Maiori, Salerno, Italy and worked as a car man for the New York, New Haven, and Hartford Railroad Companies for 40 years. He was also an Army veteran of World War I. He died in 1992 at the age of 98, and though we were never what one might call close, especially as a young boy, my grandfather made a lasting impression on me.

From what I could gather from discussions with my brothers and uncles, Grandpa was a stern taskmaster with his children and his grandchildren. He was also a proud man, who spent a great deal of time working on a small fenced-in yard, as well as in his garden and grapevines. He was the quintessential immigrant, who came to this country without a family or money and through a work ethic that characterized many people of his generation, earned a place as a recipient of the American dream. He married, bought a home, raised a family and saved his money. He also retained a great deal of his native culture and tried to pass it along to his children.

Like many people, he was protective of his possessions, especially the aforementioned garden, lawn, and grapevines. He was always weeding, picking out rocks, or, more commonly, yelling at the neighborhood kids to stay off the grass. In discussions with family members about him, I have heard them say two things: I was his favorite and he suffered from severe bouts of mental illness. (Some might say that his affection for me was a sign of mental illness, but I would take exception to that point of view.)

Although I was too young to recall these events myself, my brothers, uncles, and mother have told me that I was the only one who would be allowed to water the grass or to work in the garden with him or to watch him when he made wine.

What has to be remembered about all of this, however, is that our neighborhood was already in a state of decline. The fact that anyone had grass growing in their yard was an amazing feat. My grandfather was also said to be a bit of a tyrant. I remember my brothers recounting stories of how he would keep pellet guns (or BB guns as they were called then) strategically placed in different corners of his apartment so that if anyone found themselves roaming too far into his territory, a volley or two would remind the young person to move to a different locale.

As I mentioned, we lived in the apartment on the first floor. My maternal grandmother had passed away in the early 1960s and my grandfather remained in the home until he was hospitalized in the 1980s. My existence here was neither peaceful nor affluent. We were poor. The neighborhood was full of teens with whom my brothers associated. They might even be called a gang, although from my recollection, it was more of a *near group* than a gang [Yablonsky 1957]. They liked to call themselves the *Frank Street Gang*, but essentially, they all gathered in certain places, sometimes vandalized or stole property, or perhaps found beer or hard liquor to consume. They had no gang colors, rituals, or other symbols of organized gang activity. Membership was based largely on living in the neighborhood and whether or not some sort of favorable relationship existed between the person and the members of the group. This is not unusual, since most researchers on gangs and gang behavior have difficulty coming up with a concise definition. I think much of the confusion that has arisen in the gang literature, as well as the public's perception of gang behavior, is due to the interchangeable use of the term "gang" and "group."

As I will describe in another chapter, there are a wide variety of gangs, with different characteristics and purposes, with some focusing on turf, others on making money, still others on gaining status through the use of violence or even graffiti (see, for instance, Klein and Maxson [1989]; Miller [1990]; Cohen [1955]; Spergel [1989]; Hagedorn [1988]; Huff [1990]; and Klein, Maxson, and Miller [1995]).

I was on the receiving end of quite a bit of abuse from the neighborhood kids, largely because I was smaller and younger than everyone else. In fact, while we lived on Frank Street, there were few kids my age who lived there. And while my brother's friends knew they could only go so far in terms of harassing me, my brothers gave themselves free reign to hassle me. Somehow it was okay for them to beat and tease me, but if anyone else strayed beyond the bounds of acceptable behavior, they would collectively come to my rescue. As a result, the older kids in the neighborhood were careful around me.

There was one exception to this rule. Franky Vollmer lived two houses away from us. Franky was a big kid who could probably have squashed anyone in the neighborhood had he the inclination, but Franky was mentally challenged, albeit slightly. He talked slowly and sometimes stuttered, and he was clumsy in his movements. While kids can be cruel, and this group was no exception, they also loved him dearly. In the same way the guys protected me, they looked out for Franky's welfare as well. Franky was always kind to me and used to spend time playing with me when all the other kids in the neighborhood were off doing their own thing. Years later Franky went to work for my mother at the nursing home as a cook. He and I spent lots of time together playing cards on his breaks, and I would help out in the kitchen when he was cooking. He was a good man and although I lost touch with him when I left New Haven, my brother Mark recently learned that he died of cancer a few years ago. I think of him a lot lately.

Like most kids, the games we played revolved around the professional sports seasons. In the fall, we could be found playing tackle football in the street. This made the injury rate increase significantly, especially when my brother Brad played. I used to watch him line up the runner so that when he tackled him, the boy got slammed into Brad on one side and a parked car on the other. Later, when I started to play, I realized that this was actually an effective way to keep the offense from running in that direction. Since the street was rather narrow, especially because of the parked cars, it was relatively easy to figure out which direction they were going to run or pass. Thanks to Brad, I became fairly adept at playing this game, which meant I was frequently included as a member. As any kid will admit, getting picked last is humiliating. I was given that distinction for a long time, because I was so much smaller and younger than everyone else. Once I grew a little and learned from the others, I soon found myself higher up on the choice list.

I also learned how to use the natural obstacles to create a "pick" on the defensive player. For instance, I would run down the street and veer on to the sidewalk. The person defending me would inevitably follow and I would quickly turn and run around a tree, thereby freeing myself for the pass. The defender had no choice but to go around the tree or to stop and circle around the other way. In either case, I was open and caught many passes. I did the same thing with parked cars. I would get my opponent to run around the car and then I would swing out into the middle of the street, with my defenders several steps behind me. This became a real problem when I played with older kids who were embarrassed by my chicanery. Suddenly the sidewalk became out of bounds, and it was an "illegal procedure" to run around or over the parked cars—the big babies.

In the spring, we played baseball. Because we could not afford the equipment nor did we have access to a baseball field, we improvised a bit. Instead of a baseball, we would take a couple of white socks and bunch them together, inside one another, to form a tight sphere. Then we would take black electrical tape and wrap it around the socks. This became our baseball. If we were hit with an inside fast ball, it did not matter since it was not as hard as a conventional baseball (and inside pitches and "bean balls" were part of the game). Because a conventional wooden bat would not be effective, we found plastic ones, also known as "wiffle bats," named after the game. Instead of bases, we used landmarks: old man Bodie's car was first base, the manhole cover was second, the sewer grate was third, and the lid of a garbage can or sometimes a piece of cardboard, served as home plate. Losing the ball presented few problems: if it were to roll down the sewer or somehow get lost, all we needed to do was to find a couple of socks and the electrical tape. It was a great way to pass the time.

In fact, my brothers spent hours imitating Mickey Mantle and other baseball legends. I was still a little too young to play with them, but when they were shorthanded (and desperate) they would let me play catcher or some other position where I could not cause any damage. Once in a while they would even let me try my hand at hitting. Actually, I had good hand-to-eye coordination and could hit the ball with some regularity. As I grew older and became more proficient, as with football, I was increasingly included in the games.

My father, who came from an Irish family, never played any of these games with us. I remember him as a stern man, who worked hard and had a clear view of how life should be. In his view, one grew up, found a job, got married and raised a family. This was a traditional view of life held by many people of his generation. He was also an autocrat and intolerant of many things. In conversations with my brothers about him, they recount stories of a stubbornness that few have ever matched.

In my own case, I was told that as a child, my father wanted all of his sons to be right-handed. To be left-handed was somehow awkward, unusual, or strange. Thus, while my brothers had little problem adjusting to this lesson, I, like my father, had my own ideas. As many times as he would put the spoon in my right hand at the dinner table, I would switch it to my left one. So intent on my being right-handed, my father actually tried to prevent me from using my left hand by restraining it during meals. My brother Brad has told me that I responded by refusing to eat and then as he put it, "bawling my head off."

My father worked for a rug company, cleaning rugs in our basement and bringing them to the customers' homes. He also worked as a toll collector on the local interstate. For a time, he worked hard to provide for his family. At some point, however, something changed. While always a man with a taste for alcohol, gradually he slipped into binges, drinking excessively. Along with this came a penchant for gambling. Unfortunately, he was not successful at this endeavor, and suddenly additional financial troubles were combined with social ones. He lost several jobs as a result of either sleeping while on duty, reporting for work inebriated, or simply not showing up at all.

There was usually some scandal associated with a number of these jobs. For example, while few wish to discuss it, there was a question of whether or not he was involved in some sort of scam while working at the toll booth. I recall that one of my father's most annoying habits was that he would keep change in his pocket and jingle it as he walked. Given that the job did not pay well, and given the dire financial straits we found ourselves in, I always wondered how he managed to have a pocket full of change. Perhaps there was some truth to the allegations.

Added to this was the fact that my father was not what one would call saintly. He was a hustler; one who dabbled in a lot of legal and quasi-legal activities. As such, it would not be a terrible surprise to learn that he pushed the boundaries of acceptable behavior in many instances.

My father was also a huge fan of the actor Jackie Gleason. He regularly watched the show *The Honeymooners* and even imitated the behavior of the Gleason's character, Ralph Kramden. This character was a bus driver who struggled to earn a living in a cold water flat in New York with his wife, Alice, played by Audrey Meadows. Their best friends and neighbors were the Nortons, Trixie and Ed, played by Joyce Randolph and Art Carney.

Norton was a dimwitted but lovable character who worked for the Department of Public Works in the sewer. His wife Trixie was Alice's best friend and confidante. The show depicted life during this period of American society and showed their struggles and the tribulations in the pursuit of the American dream. Parenthetically, the cartoon *The Flintstones* was based on Jackie Gleason and *The Honeymooners*.

My father idolized Ralph Kramden. I think in a way he identified with Ralph, and this made his imitative behavior easier to understand. He would strut around the house demanding things from everyone in the same fashion Ralph did on the show. The impact of this type of behavior was not lost on his youngest two sons. Years later this type of modeling repeated itself in my brother Daryl, who became enamored with the character George Jefferson of the show *The Jeffersons*. George was an African American who struggled to succeed in the projects of New York. He worked hard and became successful and was able to "move on up" the ladder of success, as the theme song depicts. The problem was that George was a racist who did not want anything to do with his white neighbors and who struggled to find his identity as a wealthy man with roots as a poor African American. The show was a comedy in which situations would arise that George would handle badly or exacerbate, largely because he, like Kramden, saw the world as a dichotomous variable. It was one way or the other: his views were the correct ones and everyone else's were wrong.

As a man in his late twenties to his early thirties, Daryl had a tendency to strut like George Jefferson, to hold racist views just as George did, and in some cases, actually quoted him by mimicking his voice. Unfortunately, like my father before him, Daryl was unable to separate comedic depictions, which in some cases were tragic characterizations, from real life. To them, the world *was* as Ralph Kramden and George Jefferson believed it to be. While Daryl and my father would scoff at this conclusion, I really believe they began to see the world through the characters' eyes and lost the ability to deal with the objective world.

If my father was the loudmouth show off, who was typically belligerent with people and abusive to his children, my mother was just the opposite. Like my father, she came from an immigrant family, although in her case it was Italian rather than Irish. She was raised in a traditional home, in which gender roles were clearly defined. As the only girl in a family of four children, she learned that the good wife was the passive one.

Moreover, having grown up in a traditional Italian home, where issues of manhood and masculinity are clearly defined, when those issues presented themselves in our family, they stood clearly within the parameters of cultural expectations. Those same standards prohibited any intervention on her part even if she did not agree with them. Thus, to say she was not a strong woman is somewhat of an understatement: to say that she fit squarely within the traditions of her culture, both married and native, would accurately describe her behavior. She was dependent in every sense of the word, economically, socially, and emotionally.

Years later this would become the explanation for her postdivorce behavior, especially as it related to her children. In my view, I believe she simply gave up and decided to assert some independence for the first time in her life. The consequences of this, however, meant that she effectively abandoned her children and her responsibilities as a parent.

Like my father's childhood, which consisted of nine boys and three girls, in which traditional Irish views of femininity and masculinity were enforced, as well as my grandfather's house, which held similar attitudes, our house of four boys was one in which sentiment or emotions, other than anger and aggressiveness, were not tolerated. As the youngest, and by definition, the smallest member of the family, much of the adolescent displays of bullying were practiced on me. My father looked upon these events, which became routine, as rites of passage into manhood. This kind of physical abuse was supposed to toughen me up. As he would tell me when I was 10 years old, I was "half a man" and that I should stand up to anyone who blocked my path. As I grew older and *he* became my obstacle, I have always wondered if his views began to change, especially when I became strong enough to defend myself.

At any rate, as a young boy, one of my favorite shows was *Lassie*. Every Sunday night the show would appear and it would end with Lassie raising her paw as a way of saying good-bye. Unfortunately, for some reason this act wreaked havoc with my emotions. As I watched while laying on a blanket, with my head propped up on a pillow facing the television, I would invariably begin to cry. To the "men" of the McNamara family, this was perceived as a weakness. As such, each week I would be pelted with assorted objects and mugged at the end of every show. In fact, my brothers would wait with great anticipation to see if I would become emotional at the conclusion of the show and then pounce when the moment invariably arrived. I do not blame them for this: they were simply trying to live up to the expectations that were set out by our father. And to be honest, I do not blame him either. This is a cultural and social class trait that developed as a means of survival.

As the years progressed, I became a bit older and a bit tougher. I was also able to fight back a bit better, although any reasonable person knows that the chance of winning against three opponents is small, especially when they live in the same house. Any claimed victory would be a small one and avenged a short time later. Occasionally however, I snuck a good punch in and had a chance to run away.

Academic Talent

After a period of time, we began a series of relocations. First, we moved to a house on Howard Avenue. It was a home instead of an apartment and I believe the space issue was a factor in this decision. The house was seven or eight blocks away from Frank Street and I found myself in a different school district. At my old school, Truman Elementary, I was following in the great tradition of the trouble making and fighting McNamaras. My brothers had preceded me at the school and by the time I arrived, our family name was well known to the administrators. Thus, even in kindergarten, I was given some attention.

The new school had, perhaps for me, the most significance. Horace Day School was located just at the end of the street, less than a block away. I was to spend second and third grade there and it was here I met some of the most influential people in my young life. I also discovered that I was one of perhaps two or three students who were white, the remaining students were a mixture of various racial and ethnic minorities. It was not long before I was a friend to many of the students, however, mixing freely with all sorts of different children. It was in this school that I learned two essential things about myself: I was interested in reading and I had the ability to get people involved in things.

While I was in the third grade at Horace Day, I also acquired a bit of culture. A friend of mine, I'll call him Charlie, used to play the coronet in the school band. It was not really a band, it was more like a group of people who got together with a teacher who tried to teach them how to play their instruments. They were not very good, and there were often more people than instruments. (Sharing a mouthpiece and spit is one way to find out who your friends really are.) I decided I wanted to learn how to play the coronet. I had no background, I could not read music, I did not even know that the instruments came in cases. But I gave it my best effort and even learned a little about music. Unfortunately, when my fellow musicians and I returned to school the following September, we found that the teacher had been laid off, all the instruments sent to another school, and our music room had become storage space.

It was also during this time that the SRA program was being implemented in my school. SRA Reading Laboratories are prepackaged materials for individualized practice of reading skills. SRAs are short stories or articles printed on laminated cards. These stories and articles are arranged progressively in order of difficulty and are color coded for easy recognition by the children. The colors begin with red, then progress to orange, gold, brown, tan, lime, green, olive, aqua, blue, purple, and finally violet. Skill exercises and/or questions follow each story.

After selecting a card, the child tests him- or herself on comprehension, records his or her performance in a record book, and moves on to the next story and exercise. SRAs are an individualized reading program in that they allow for self-selection, self-pacing, and self-evaluation. Since that time, serious reading research indicates that a great deal more is learned when children discuss stories with peers, or when children read real books and write essays, rather than when they learn bits and pieces or fill in the blanks. As most teachers will argue, there is a difference between teaching and testing. When children "do" SRAs they are being tested and receive little or no instruction. Teaching involves helping, guiding, demonstrating, modeling, and explaining. In short, it involves children and teachers interacting as they find ways to construct meaning from text. This can hardly be accomplished when kids sit by themselves at desks and work alone.

Of course, this information was unknown at the time. The SRA publishers had conducted some research on their program and found it to be quite successful. (This finding is now a dubious one.) In my case, I thought it was great. I had the chance to sit at my desk and read as much as I wanted. I also learned that I was pretty far advanced from the other kids. I quickly outpaced everyone in the class and began to wonder what would happen when I finished the sequence. I had hoped there was another, but after my music experience I began to wonder if I would have to leave the school after I had finished the set. As a result, I slowed down. I did not read as quickly nor as many stories. Rather, I turned my attention to sports.

The Organizer

I decided that the school needed a football team that could play other schools, such as Truman Elementary, located a few blocks away. I got some of my friends together and they agreed it would be a lot of fun. We had been playing against each other for so long that it was kind of boring. I wrote a letter to the third-grade teacher at Truman, which essentially challenged the class to a game (I did not learn anything about diplomacy until I was much older).

We did not get a response, so one day a few of us snuck out of school early and walked over to Truman to talk to some of the kids about the game. The teacher found us and told us to leave and threatened to have us kicked out of school. The next day I got called into the principal's office, a place where people knew me by my first name.

The principal, Mr. Panicino, used to be a teacher at Truman. He was also familiar with the McNamara family: during his tenure at Truman school, he had the pleasure of having all three of my brothers as students in his class. Daryl was the one who was most vivid in his memory and when he saw me sitting outside his office, he was quick to point out that he was tired of dealing with us and, as principal, he would not tolerate any transgressions from me. I remember him telling me that if he had to, he would "kick my ass all the way to the harbor" if I did not, as he put it, "straighten up and fly right." I thought he was angry because we had left school early. I had done this before and it had not generated this kind of reaction, and I said as much. He thought I was being insolent, and perhaps it sounded that way. I just wanted to know what made him so angry.

During the course of the conversation he told me that organizing a gang was the best way to get expelled and to lead to a life of crime. I tried to tell him that I was only trying to organize a football game, but he would not believe me. Apparently, our trip to Truman school was interpreted by the teacher to mean that we were looking to beat up other kids. She then called Mr. Panicino and told him what she thought had happened. I could not convince him that all we wanted was a chance to play a game against some kids in another neighborhood.

This ended any chance of getting an organized league together and I spent a lot of time pounding the chalk out of erasers as a result. I still hate chalk dust and to this day I think of Horace Day School and clapping every eraser in the school as punishment for attempting to organize a gang that did not exist. As I was serving out my sentence, I thought I had been treated unfairly and wanted to exact a bit of revenge on someone. As I clapped the erasers in front of a large open window on the third floor of the building, I noticed that the window overlooked one of the entrances to the school. I watched as visitors, maintenance people, students, and administrators passed by below me and I could not resist the temptation to "drop" a few erasers out of the window. I laid several on the window sill, to give the impression that I was diligently performing my duties, and if one happened to slip off and fall three stories to the ground, it would obviously be perceived as accidental. The fact that the erasers landed quite a distance away from the window was immaterial. I was having a lot of fun sniping at people with my chalk-filled erasers when my last victim was none other than Mr. Panicino. I managed to land a white rectangle full of chalk right on the top of his shiny bald head. I did not know it was him until he looked up at me and saw me laughing hysterically. I paid for that mistake. I spent the next several weeks sweeping the hall, picking up garbage around the school, and emptying every trash can in the school. But it was an accident... really.

Can We Take the Ghetto Out of the Boy?

What seemed like a day or two later (actually it was closer to a year) we moved again, this time to Chichester, an affluent town in Connecticut. As I understand it, my brother Mark had been attacked by a vicious watch dog at an auto parts store. He was seriously injured and my parents sued the company. With the settlement money, they purchased a home in a better neighborhood.

I did not want to leave my friends nor did I know much about this area other than it was farther from New Haven than I wanted to be. The people in Chichester were different from the ones to which I was accustomed. For instance, one of the most striking differences was that most of the people were white. I was used to being one of the only white students in the schools and the only one in my neighborhood. In contrast, in Chichester schools there was usually only a single African American or Hispanic student.

Another difference was that the people in our new neighborhood were from a higher socioeconomic status than my family. Our neighborhood was by no means affluent, and by Chichester's standards were working-class or poor families, yet they were a leap forward in social standing from us. As such, our family got into a lot of fights with our neighbors, especially Daryl and I.

Unfortunately, we were used to settling disputes in a more physical way. As a result, we were usually in trouble in school, as well as with many of the neighboring families. By this time, my brothers Brad and Mark were in their teens and had transportation. They were always mechanically inclined and were able to cannibalize enough abandoned or scrap yard vehicles to get their own car(s) on the road. Daryl was about 13 at the time and became really interested in setting fires in the woods near our house.

My father worked for a time at each of our schools as a custodian. He was happy to have this job, in part because he could keep an eye on us. However, it mattered little. Daryl continued to get into trouble, while I was only a little more creative, which made it more difficult to prove I was the culprit. Nevertheless, our standard of living had not changed: we were a dirty, unkempt, and unruly lot. We rarely had any food and when it was available, it was usually divided according to Darwin's theory. For me, there were few options except to steal what I could from other people's homes, from pharmacies, and local grocery stores. I was fortunate to be given a used bicycle for my birthday and this allowed me to roam the town at will.

While the climate had changed, as did the school, the extreme poverty did not. Nor did the lack of sensitivity on the part of my family. I am a bit embarrassed to describe the details of this story, largely because it is telling about every one of the participants and partly because I know my brothers feel guilty about it.

Like most kids my age, I had a favorite stuffed animal that was my constant companion. At some point my brothers decided that it was unmanly for a 9-year-old boy to play with a teddy bear. They would take it away from me and hide it, only to discover that I was able to retrieve it from their hiding place. Finally, in true McNamara style, they decided to make a spectacle of the situation. My oldest brother Brad had recently purchased an archery set. Setting the teddy bear on the inside wall at the end of our garage, my brothers forced me to watch the vicious execution of a defenseless teddy bear. Time after time, they practiced their archery skills, all three taking turns trying to impale my stuffed friend on a wooden arrow. Although not the most accurate, they managed to succeed. With the parting words to the effect that no one in this family was going to be a sissy, they sent me on my way and disposed of the bear. I never forgave them for their insensitivity.

While it may not seem that important to most people, what has to be remembered was that I knew this group was not the typical, garden variety family. I tried to imitate the behavior of people who I thought were "normal" and having a favorite stuffed animal was a way to do that. And although I had my share of fights and learned how to survive in this neighborhood, I still felt it was important to try to do the things that most kids did. Little did I know that there was more adversity to come my way.

My time spent in Chichester was also noteworthy because a year later, my eldest brother, perhaps feeling guilty about the teddy bear incident, gave me a puppy, whom I promptly named Bandit. We already had another dog, one that epitomized the concept of loyalty and toughness, Duke. This was a street dog personified. He was a mixed breed, but he was well-trained and would not hesitate to attack on command or if he perceived any type of threat. This came in handy when older kids decided they wanted to take revenge on me after they had traded blows with Daryl.

The introduction of Bandit to the equation really did not go over that well. As I recall, Duke wanted no part of him and neither did anyone else in the house. I was told the dog would be my total responsibility. Unfortunately, we often had no money for our own food, let alone for the dog. Thus, the dog lasted about a month before my father decided to give him away to someone else. That is, of course, without telling me.

What was especially interesting at this point in my life was that, while my brothers spent a lot of their free time teaching me what it was like to be a boxer's heavy bag, I found I would not tolerate that type of treatment from anyone else. My brothers showed me how to fight, mostly by being the victim, but they also tried to instill in me a sense of pride and independence. I do not think they recognized these episodes as lessons: rather I think they looked upon them as ways to "toughen" up their little brother. The problem was that I had inherited my family's sense of stubbornness. Thus, as many times as they tried to make me act the way they wanted, or to do the things they wanted me to do, if I was not interested, I would not budge. If I had been able to learn about diplomacy at an earlier age, I would not have had to endure so many bruises. I was told by relatives and other family friends that even as a child, I had my own way of looking at things and would not heed the counsel or commands of others.

As a sociologist I am supposed to argue that this was due to environmental circumstances and situational inducements. I cannot say in good conscience that this was entirely the case, however. I feel that biological factors do play a role in shaping people's behavior and attitudes. I do not know to what extent or even which is most pervasive, but I believe that the combination of those factors explains a lot more of a person's actions than any one by itself. This is especially true with regard to my own situation.

By all rights, if the environment dictated a person's attitudes and behavior, I should have become the racist, sexist, and macho-driven moron that characterized many members of my family during that period. I did not. I believed that people could do anything they wanted to. If a boy wanted to have a stuffed animal as his best friend, so what? If a girl wanted to be a construction worker, a doctor, or President of the United States, I wanted to know why she could not be allowed. Of course, this perspective, even as a child, was met with swift and severe retaliation by my family, especially my father. In that kind of environment, there was no place for these types of thoughts.

As I mentioned, despite the physical and emotional abuse that my family inflicted, I had no tolerance for anyone else laying a hand on me. I got into a lot of fights because of comments people made about me, tried to intimidate me, or simply did or said something that sent me over the edge. One day two of my best friends, who were brothers and lived right next door to us, were playing baseball and as is often the case with adolescents, an argument broke out over a called play at the plate. Words were exchanged and the younger of the two made the mistake of pushing me to the ground from behind.

To grasp the significance of this story, it must be understood that of all the people I had come to know in this town, these two boys were the ones I trusted the most. I cared little for the others and the hostilities between myself and them were legendary. In short, I would fight anyone at any time, in any setting, for virtually any reason. The only exception to this were the two brothers. In fact, I became involved in my share of fights in an effort to protect them from harm. There were several instances in which they encountered trouble with some of the neighborhood kids, who promptly used their larger numbers to overwhelm them.

Parenthetically, during my time spent in this town I learned a few things about myself. First, I hated bullies and would pick a fight with them just to teach them a lesson. Second, I despised arrogant people, and would do my best to humiliate them when they acted as though they were better than everyone else. Third, I felt that most of the time people did not play fair. This was true in games, in school, and especially, when they were afraid. I also learned from my past experiences with my brothers that there was no such thing as a "fair fight." When fists begin to fly, the rules generally go out the window. (This was a problem when I later became involved in the martial arts. In sparring tournaments, the rules are clearly defined and the fighting is controlled. I had a hard time learning those lessons.)

In conflicts with Eddie and Dave, a group of kids typically joined in the fracas as soon as they learned that it was unlikely they would be harmed. Eddie and Dave could handle themselves fairly well; however, in one particular case, they were simply overwhelmed. After running to the scene and trying to drag nearly a dozen kids off the two boys, I decided to use a bit of strategy. I ran to my house and retrieved Duke, the wonder dog. I grabbed his leash and decided it would be a good time to take him for a walk to the exact location of the fight.

It was years later that this scene flashed into my mind when I was working as a security guard at an amusement park that tended to attract outlaw bikers. There is nothing that will stop a bar fight faster than the introduction of an aggressive dog. Duke was the quintessential fighter and everyone in our neighborhood knew it. In fact, many of their pets had suffered a painful fate as a result of taking him on in a fight. When I trotted the dog to the area, the fight broke up immediately. I then proceeded to take the dog and my two friends back to my house. To me, that was the ultimate act of loyalty. That I would risk my own neck to save a buddy. We exacted our revenge the next day at the bus stop. Unknown to Eddie, Dave, or myself, Duke had somehow gotten out of the house and was sitting by a bush nearby. His vantage point made it easy for the others to see him, but we did not notice it. We were told about this later, but at the time we simply thought that the kids were sorry for what they had done and let us retaliate by hitting them a few times.

There were many such instances in which our bonds of friendship were strengthened. Another instance that I will never forget occurred in the playground of our neighborhood school. We were riding our bikes by the basketball courts and using the hilly landscape as ramps to see how far we could jump. A few other kids came and began teasing a large white dog that lived next door to the school. The dog was kept in a fenced-in area that ran around the school property. The kids were teasing the dog with sticks and some started to throw clumps of dirt at the dog, what we used to call "dirt bombs." As we stopped to tell the kids to leave the dog alone, a large man suddenly appeared with his two sons and began to chase the kids around, screaming at them. He caught a few and slapped them across their faces. His two sons grabbed me, threw me off my bike and the father proceeded to slap me across the face and then allowed the sons to pummel me with punches to the stomach and groin area. I collapsed on the ground gasping for air while the man towered over me and yelled a variety of expletives and threatened to kill me and everyone else if we did not leave his dog alone. As I looked around I saw about five other kids holding their faces and crying. I assumed that they had been slapped as I had. Eddie and Dave helped me up and took me back to their house and told their father what had happened.

Their father became enraged and called the police. The man was subsequently arrested and convicted of assault and risk of injury to a minor. I felt somewhat vindicated, but I would have loved to see Daryl, Brad, and

Mark spend a little time alone with him. However, the point is that Eddie and Dave were there for me.

However, months later, on the day that Dave pushed me from behind, he was forever placed into another category. Here was someone who I trusted, had fought with and had felt was my best friend, who betrayed me. In a scene that Daryl described as one of the funniest he has ever witnessed, after getting up off the ground, Eddie and Dave were on either side of me. As the fight began, I turned and pushed Eddie as hard as I could and then turned and began fighting with Dave. When I heard Eddie coming back, I kicked Dave in the groin and turned to fight with Eddie. Just as Dave was recovering enough to continue, I kicked Eddie in the knee, which sent him sprawling and landed a solid left hook to his temple. He went down and began to cry. Dave saw this and became enraged. As he charged, I sidestepped and threw him in the direction of his brother. They became tangled in a pile of legs and arms and finally relented. We made up some time that week but it was never the same for me again. I felt that when the chips were down, they would be there for me. I was wrong. It was at this point that I learned perhaps my most valuable lesson. It was important, because in the coming years I was to experience quite a bit of adversity and disappointment. Eddie and Dave taught me that I could never rely on anyone for anything at any time. It was really a day of reckoning for me.

Like my relationship with Eddie and Dave, I came to the conclusion that even though they were my family, I could not count on them for much. This was difficult for a 10-year-old to grasp and was exacerbated by the fact that of all my relatives, the only one I really admired and cared about at that time was Mark. He was my favorite and the one I looked up to. This image would also be shattered a few years later, which left me angry at myself for failing to remember my golden rule. While I was heartbroken at what had happened, I was disappointed in myself for trusting anyone and vowed never to let it happen again.

The Subculture of Violence

During the next few months of 1970, the situation at home grew worse. My mother and father continued to argue and fight, there was more tension and hostility in the house than ever before, and the situation continued to deteriorate. My mother decided that she was going to apply for a job to pay the bills, a claim to which my father reacted violently. This had become a common feature in the McNamara household, and given that my brothers were in high school, they began to physically stand up to my father. These physical confrontations would not end in a standoff: remember all the parties in this household had been trained from an early age that the solution to a problem often involved one's fists. This was an acceptable, and even expected, way to solve one's problems. Failure to do so would lead to the perception that one was weak and easily exploited. Years later, when I first learned of what Marvin Wolfgang and Franco Ferracutti [1967] termed "the subculture of violence," I realized they were talking about my family. Violence in this subculture is not immoral in any way, because it fits within the community standards of acceptable behavior. According to the theory, the use of violence simply becomes a part of one's daily life, and it is a means by which problems are solved and personal honor is preserved.

Thus, I saw an increase in the number of violent episodes, as well as an escalation in the level of violence. No longer were my brothers and my father content to simply push and shove each other, all the while castigating one another with insults and profanity. As time went on, they became all-out brawls, leaving the participants cut and bruised and in many cases, bleeding.

When my mother announced that she was going to get a job, the reaction was angry and swift. I should also add that by this time my father was clearly an alcoholic and a compulsive gambler, who thought nothing of spending his paycheck either in a bar, at a race track, or both. He still tried to maintain the image that he was the head of the household, that he was in charge, and most important, that he was the sole breadwinner. In his mind, the fact that his wife went to work implied that he was unable to support his family. Although this was a true and accurate picture, his cultural standards simply would not allow him to accept that fact. His brothers and sisters drank, but they were able to keep things together, as did his father and mother. In his mind, especially as one of the oldest in his family, he could not live with the cloud of failure that my mother's job represented.

This was perhaps the first time that my mother had asserted herself. To her credit, she defied her own cultural standards and broke many gender stereotypes. In retrospect, this was a courageous thing to do, although I am not convinced it was solely for altruistic reasons. I believe she simply had had enough of her relationship with my father and was tired of dealing with a chaotic situation. In short, I think she took the job under the guise that it was to feed her children, but in reality she used it as an escape. Despite the extra income, there was no increase in the amount of food, the bills continued to mount, with creditors calling on a regular basis, and her relationship with her boss at the diner where she worked took a romantic turn. This leads me to believe that she was searching for a way out. Ultimately she found it, but she was still saddled with the responsibilities of her children. That too, would be resolved in the coming years, but initially the break came when she filed for divorce.

The Breakup

For me, the news of the divorce meant little: no one really explained what was going on or how it would affect me. I think by that point, everyone was scrambling to find some way to control the damage it inflicted on them as individuals. I cannot really blame them, especially Brad and Mark, who I think were treated unfairly. Fortunately, they were close to one another and had the chance to lean on each other emotionally, socially, and economically for support. This is not to say they had it easy, however.

These were 16- or 17-year-old kids who were essentially told that they were emancipated minors and were forced to earn a living on their own without anyone's help. This was not exactly an improvement over their current conditions because, at least in Chichester, they had a place to sleep. While relationships between them and my father were not exactly cordial, at least they could avoid my parents and have a place to wash their clothes and sleep on a regular basis. Now even that was being taken away from them.

My brothers have told me that they felt guilty for not being able to do more for me when things deteriorated. To this day they tell me that of all of us, I had it the worst. I submit that by all accounts I had it easy compared to what they were forced to endure. While what I experienced was not exactly a picture-perfect childhood, I believe I had the ability to adapt and the firm belief that I had done nothing wrong. I also believed that anything was better than the conditions that existed in that house. I am not certain my brothers had that same level of conviction. In fact, I think that some of the guilt they have experienced comes from the fact that they felt others were willing to help them, but no one was really willing to help me or Daryl. I cannot speak for Daryl, who was 14 at the time, and well on his way to being on a first name basis with the local police department, but I suspect he too has had difficulty resolving a number of issues that occurred during this time.

For me, I somehow knew I would be okay. I never had the destructive tendencies that Daryl had, rather I had in me a kind of resolve that I would survive this obstacle as I had many others in the past. I remember thinking, "What could be worse? I am in a situation in which there is no food, people are always fighting with one another, my parents do not really care about me, they are more interested in themselves than anything else, and my brothers are always pounding the hell out of me. What could be worse than that?" Well, to be honest, I was wrong. In the coming four years I learned that there were many things far worse than that. I was exposed to the negative aspects of humanity and some of the most selfish and despicable individuals our society has to offer. What made them so loathsome was that they tried to give the appearance of propriety. That is, they appeared to be cordial, caring, and wonderful people, but their motivations were based on greed, money, and/or ego. Thus, while I thought things might have been turning for the better, the problems were really only beginning.

References

Cohen, A. K. (1955). *Delinquent boys: The culture of the gang.* New York: The Free Press.

Doomhoff G. W. (1978). *Who really rules?* London: Transaction.

Hagedorn, J. (1988). *People and folks: Gangs, crime and the underclass in a rustbelt city*. Chicago, IL: Lakeview Press.

Huff, C. R. (Ed.). (1990). *Gangs in America*. Newbury Park, CA: Sage Publishers.

Klein, M., & Maxson, C. (1989). Street gang violence. In N. A. Weiner & M. E. Wolfgang (Eds.), *Violent crime, violent criminals* (pp. 198-234). Newbury Park, CA: Sage Publishers.

Klein, M., Maxson, C., & Miller, J. (1995). *The modern gang reader.* Los Angeles: Roxbury.

Miller, W. (1990). Why the United States has failed to solve its youth gang problem. In C. R. Huff (Ed.), *Gangs in America* (pp. 263-287). Newbury Park, CA: Sage Publishers.

Powledge, F. (1970). *Model city.* New York: Simon and Schuster.

Spergel, I. (1989). Youth gangs: Continuity and change. In N. Morris & M. Tonry (Eds.) *Crime and justice: An annual review of research,* Vol. 12. Chicago, IL: University of Chicago Press.

Talbot, A. R. (1967). *The mayor's game.* New York: Harper and Row.

U.S. Department of Commerce, Bureau of the Census. (1960). *Census of the Population,* Vol. 1, Part 8: Connecticut. Washington, DC: Author.

U.S. Department of Commerce, Bureau of the Census. 1970. *Census of the Population,* Vol. 1, Part 8: Connecticut. Washington, DC: Author.

Wolfgang, M., & Ferracutti, F. (1967). *The subculture of violence.* London: Tavistock.

Yablonsky, L. (1957). The gang as a near group. *Social Problems 7*, 108-117.

3

Divorce, Desertion, and Desperation

After my parents split up, the house in Chichester was sold and the family fragmented. I did not seé much of my brothers for a long time. They were still in school and working various part-time jobs. My father's side of the family remained lower to working class, composed of a few hard workers mixed with a healthy dose of miscreants, most of whom spent a great deal of time in bars drinking away what little money they earned. On the other hand, my mother's three brothers were rather prosperous. This was probably due to the financial support my grandfather gave them and they were able to live quite comfortably. One uncle, Tom, went on to earn an Ed.D, or an advanced degree in education. For a time he was a principal in one school district, and then served as superintendent of schools in another, but I had not seen him since I was a small boy.

It seemed clear to me, even at 10 years old, that my father's family did not like my three brothers and me, because we were my mother's children, from THAT side of the family. And my mother's family did not like us for the same reason: we were my father's children. To be fair, two of my uncles did help Brad and Mark in their time of need. I have no idea what motivated them, but they deserve some credit for helping them. Each uncle continued to have some sort of relationship with them as they progressed into adulthood. Recently however, those relations have cooled considerably.

With my mother's family, I felt that my uncles and their families always looked down on us because we were so poor. I cannot speak for my brothers, but I know that when we visited I felt as though I were an animal that had to be allowed in the house, but ignored after that. On my father's side of the family, I was also treated with a lack of respect. The only difference was that with my Irish cousins, we settled our disputes much more physically. I recall many arguments with my cousins that culminated in the use of rakes, shovels, bricks, or any other implement that was handy. When I attempted to settle the problems with my mother's family in the same way, the parents intervened and I was punished for being uncivilized. In short, my brothers and I were usually, and I felt always, treated like second- or third-class citizens. Every time we visited them, I felt that they expected us to thank them for all they had done for us.

The Kimberly Spa

After the divorce, I first began living in an apartment with my mother but for some reason, I was told this was not going to work out. This was the beginning of a series of moves from one parent to the other, which I will come back to in a minute. I suspect that the reason I had to leave initially had more to do with the situation involving my mother's boss, with whom she had been having an extramarital affair for some time. I think I was cramping her style and she wanted some freedom. I went to live with my father for a while, but he was still drinking heavily and became abusive, to me and everyone else. Still, I thought he wanted me more than my mother did and it was a chance to see my brothers again.

At this point, it was not that I did not care about my mother, in fact I was the first to defend her when the subject of responsibility for us arose. She convinced me that it would be better if I were with my brothers. And since she could not afford to bring them with her, it made logical sense. To be honest, I missed them. I did not like Daryl much, but what 10-year-old likes his teenage brother?

This situation was not without its benefits, however. As a boy, I was afraid of Brad, I think because he was nine years older than I was. By the time our family broke up, he was nearly an adult. He also worked a lot so I did not see him much, but I know he cared a great deal for me. In fact, I think he was the one who gave me my dog Bandit. I also remember him scraping enough money together so that I could buy another used bicycle from one of the neighbors while we lived in Chichester. Still, he intimidated me at times.

One of my favorite memories was when we lived on Kimberly Avenue in New Haven. My father had rented an apartment just above the Kimberly Spa, one of his favorite bars, or "gin mills," as he used to call them. He worked for *The New Haven Register* at the time, a local newspaper. This was the only time I recall when it was easy to find him. He was either in one of two places, the bar downstairs or at the newspaper (the former more often than the latter). He even ate his meals there. The owner, an Irish women whose husband had passed away and who employed her two daughters as bartenders, used to prepare meals in a small kitchen behind the bar.

At any rate, one of my favorite things to do as a young boy happened on Friday nights. I stayed awake until Brad and/or Mark came home from work and we stayed up playing cards or watch a late night movie together. I always fell asleep before the end of the movie, but not before I had a chance to play Poker, Setback, Fish, or Gin Rummy. Sometimes they tried to bring home popcorn or some other treat. Little did I know that they were barely making any money themselves, but they always found a way to buy me something. To this day, I still look forward to Fridays, movies, and popcorn: it is one of my favorite things to do.

We lived together in this apartment for a while and I started working with my father. His job was to distribute hundreds of papers all around the city and to cover the carriers' paper routes when they could not complete their duties (e.g., vacations, illness). At that time, there were two papers, *The Journal Courier,* which was the morning edition, and *The New Haven Register,* which circulated in the afternoon. My father had the afternoon routes, which also meant early delivery on Sundays. I spent hours with my father as I jogged next to the car, tossing papers to hundreds of customers as he slowly drove down the streets of New Haven. I learned the fold-and-toss technique and perfected the toss from the passenger side of the vehicle on cold or rainy days.

For this effort, my father paid me two dollars per week. The reason for this may have been to teach his youngest son about the value of a dollar and to learn to meet his responsibilities; however, I believe it had more to do with convenience than to teach me one of life's important lessons. With my help, he did not have to get out of the car himself and he finished his route more quickly, which allowed him to head for the Kimberly Spa, Riley's, or some other watering hole.

The situation in the apartment was similar to the one in Chichester: there was no food in the house, the place was in shambles, and everyone was on their own. This may have been easier for Brad and Mark, and to some extent Daryl, but the options were limited for a 10-year-old. As a result, I began stealing food from grocery stores, convenience shops, and even items from discount stores, because I could sell what I stole to buy food. I learned a lot about fencing operations during this time in my life.

It would be years later that I would recall many fond memories of kind-hearted fences as I read my first sociological account of this activity: Carl Klockars' *The Professional Fence* [1974]. I remember reading and thinking to myself, "This sounds a lot like Mr. Smith on Lombard Street, or Mr. Jones on Howard Avenue." They would give me extra money or buy me a sandwich for lunch when I was around. They were nice men and Klockars' book remains one of my favorites.

I also began spending a lot of time in the Kimberly Spa. The owner and her daughters must have felt sorry for me, because I went in when my father was not around, usually during the day or right after school, and they let me sit in one of the booths and fed me corned beef sandwiches, beef stew, or whatever else they had prepared in the kitchen. They sat and talked to me for hours about all types of things. I told them I could not pay them for the food, but they always told me they would take care of it. I was worried that they were going to charge my father for the meals, but I never heard about it. And believe me, if they had, I would have caught a serious beating. While he always had money for beer and his own needs, my father was frugal when it came to providing for his family. Perhaps he felt that it would toughen us up. After all, his family was also poor and maybe he reasoned this was a good lesson for his boys to learn.

The Tom Jones Era

During the early 1970s, the Welsh singer Tom Jones was at the height of his popularity. In fact, he even had his own variety show on television. For those who remember him, his act was a sexual one: tight pants, a bare chest with gold necklaces, and sensual dance steps, which, to be fair, required a great deal of agility. One night my father caught me acting like a typical kid on the front porch of our apartment. I had been watching the Tom Jones show and had turned up the volume and was mimicking him. When I realized he had seen what I was doing, I figured I was in for a beating.

At the moment I saw him, I assumed that the belt was going to come off and I was going to get it good. I was trapped on the porch, with nowhere to go. I could jump from the second floor, but that did not seem like a prudent thing to do. As a result, I simply kept on dancing and singing, hoping for something miraculous to happen. I remember being so scared that I had never moved so quickly in my life: had this been a track meet I probably would have set a world record.

Instead of flying into a rage and proceeding to slap me around, the usual scenario, he smiled. This made me even more afraid. I thought he had lost his mind and was absolutely insane. I can vividly remember that I stopped dancing and said aloud, "Oh shit. I'm dead." Instead he said, "Robaduski, where did you learn to dance like that?" This was his nickname for me when he was in a good mood or I had done something that pleased him. When I was in trouble, which was a lot, he called me "Mr. Robert." As soon as I heard the nickname, I knew I was going to be okay, that I endured another day without getting hit. I do not know which relieved me more.

This began the legacy of perhaps the first child impersonator of famous people. I began to entertain the Kimberly Spa crowd on a regular basis, to which the drunken patrons would applaud and buy me sodas as a reward. On Sunday nights when the Tom Jones show aired, the televisions in the bar were tuned to the appropriate station, with me perched on a stool right in front of the bar facing the television. I became a celebrity of sorts. The owners asked the company that serviced the juke box to include all of Tom Jones's records so that I could perform more easily and to a wider variety of songs.

While I enjoyed the notoriety, my brothers, the sensitive modern men that they were, took exception to my newfound fame. Suddenly my father turned his attention away from me and focused on giving them a hard time, especially Daryl. He could not do anything right. This was normal, both for him as well as for me, but now it seemed that my father took his stress and anger out exclusively on him.

At first glance, one might say this would be a good thing for me: suddenly the abuse was focused elsewhere. However, my hostile relationship with Daryl took an even more aggressive turn. Everyone in the house knew what was going on: my Tom Jones act was scoring points for my father downstairs in the bar, but it meant that they had to take the heat upstairs in the apartment. In short, Daryl took his revenge on me time after time, making sure he attacked when my father was not around or sleeping off a hangover. Brad and Mark also teased me unmercifully about my starlike qualities.

After a while, I became bored with the whole affair and wanted to stop. Unfortunately, my father had other ideas. He was getting more out of this situation than anyone else. Like most people, he wanted to be able to stand out from the others, to be someone important. He could not use his job as a marker of identity, and he certainly was not wealthy by any stretch of the imagination. But he did have a son who sounded and danced like Tom Jones and people in the bar loved to watch the kid go at it. This led to a lot of backslapping and kudos for my father. Cries of "Hell of a son you've got there, Mac" were commonly heard throughout the bar. Even the owner of the bar started to take a greater interest in him. He became somebody.

When I told him that I was tired of playing the game, he would not let me quit. He told me that he would make my life miserable if I did not keep it up. He also threatened to tell my friends at school what I had been doing. This was unthinkable. Kimberly Avenue School was predominantly made up of African American students, with some Hispanics and few whites. I earned my reputation by fighting the toughest and the strongest kids there. I won, although there were times when both of us were battered and bloodied and I wondered who was actually the victor. I was not a bully, but people knew who I was and left me alone. This was not the case for the other white kids in the school. When someone was being picked on, I would sometimes intervene, especially if I thought the antagonizer was being a bully. As I said, I have always hated bullies and spent most of my life knocking them down.

Thus, my standing at school was at risk if my father let it be known that I was dancing around like a "sissy." I did not think Tom Jones was one, nor did I think that dancing made a person a sissy. In fact, there was a lot of "soul" in what he did. I could not risk the possibility of getting jammed up with my friends, however. So I kept on singing and dancing, all the while trying to figure out how to get out of the situation and how to pay my father back for his scheming ways.

At the Point of the City

At some point, I cannot adequately recall when, we moved from the apartment on Kimberly Avenue to one in the City Point section of town. I suspected that the reasons for this move had to do with my father not paying the rent. I am certain that if he could afford it, he would have stayed there forever. The setup was a perfect one for him: a job that gave him a lot of freedom, a bar a flight of stairs below him, and a group of people who thought highly of him.

I figured it out when my father lost his job at the newspaper. As with most of his jobs, it probably had to do with drinking and not performing up to standards. The worst thing that a boss could do was to give my father a lot of latitude; he needed to be supervised closely.

At any rate, we moved to an apartment right across from a little league baseball field. The water treatment plant was on the other side of the field, as was the New Haven harbor. How my father scammed his way into this apartment, I will never know. At one point, I remember my mother saying that he had been romantically involved with the landlord, a widow who lived on the first floor. I have no way of knowing if this is true, but the living situation did not change. My father continued to drink heavily and would not bring home food or other essentials.

Accustomed to scamming for food, one tactic that I used was to enter a large grocery store and act as though I had lost my mother. I then walked over to the service desk and asked whomever was working if they had seen her. I made up a name and ask them to page her over the intercom system. When she did not show up, I told them that her hearing aid must not be working, but I would find her in the store. This gave me a reason to walk around the aisles. While calling out her name I would simply stuff food in my pockets or under my clothes. We were so poor that I was forced to wear Daryl's hand-me-downs, which were quite a bit larger in size. I liked them, since they were baggy enough to store lots of food items without being noticed. I even learned to stuff a loaf of bread into my pants without being seen. Of course the bread would be crushed by the time I returned home, but it was better than nothing. We learned to make sandwiches out of condiments: ketchup, mustard, mayonnaise, even oil and vinegar (with salt and pepper of course).

Occasionally we got lucky—someone acquired lettuce and/or tomatoes and we made sandwiches out of those as well. At one point, I also started to steal canned food. I found I really liked canned beets and french-style string beans. I also learned that beef stew came in a can. My favorite kind was easy to identify: there was a huge thumb print on the top of the can.

I was caught shoplifting several times and brought to the police station. They tried to contact my father, but he was never home. Eventually, they simply brought me home and told me to stay out of trouble. Some of the officers were nice to me and actually seemed to care about my welfare. Others were just plain morons. I learned a lot more about them when I got in trouble with my friends, who were mostly African American. Even though we had done the exact same thing, they would usually treat me differently.

In fact, in some cases, I had been more involved in the event than they had, but they ended up getting slapped around or formally processed through the juvenile justice system. Now, this may be due to the fact that they knew me and thought I was basically a good kid or perhaps they were racists, or perhaps even a bit of both. In any case, I knew they were being unfair. I felt that some of the cops were little more than adult bullies.

After one such incident, I set out to avenge my friends. The idea came to me right after the first snowfall and I began to use it regularly after that. I stood on one of the many side streets that branched off from Howard Avenue and waited for a police cruiser to drive by. I had already perfected my technique on the buses that passed by, so I knew it would work. I took a rock and covered it with snow. To the casual observer, it looked like a snowball. What was more natural than a bunch of kids throwing snowballs in the street in the winter time? To a passing police officer, it was not cause for concern, even if the kids tossed a few at passing motorists. Even when the target became the police cruiser, there was no real cause for concern: just a bunch of kids having a little fun. Until the window shattered or the rock left a large dent in the door of the cruiser.

Typically, my friends and I would throw the snowball and the minute we heard the crash or the loud "thunk" I knew we had made contact. At that point, I immediately took off running down the side street trying to find a hiding place in an alley. Depending on where we were at the time, we would also run into either Kimberly field or the Armstrong Rubber Plant's field along Long Wharf Drive. The longer the police chased us, the more fun we had. My friends and I spent many afternoons pegging cars and ducking the police. Occasionally we hit a private motorist and he would chase us. Most of the time they gave up quickly, because this was not the type of neighborhood to be roaming around, especially if one was unfamiliar with the social and physical landscape. We tended to focus on the police, because we knew they would always chase us and would be zealous in their pursuits.

As I mentioned, I remained at the same school while living at City Point, which allowed me to continue to spend time with my friends. I knew I had little to go home to and school was a type of sanctuary for me. I was a fair student, but compared to some of my friends, I was a genius. Since I was proficient and was willing to help my class mates, the teachers liked me. It was years later that it occurred to me that the vast majority of the students were African American and Hispanic, but all the teachers and administrators were white. Moreover, few of them lived in or near the neighborhood. Perhaps this played a role in my relationship with them. This is pure speculation, but remember, race relations in the Elm City were never what one might call cordial, especially during the 1970s.

School also provided an outlet for me. It was the only time I could remember being happy. While certainly not the most popular kid in school, I knew most of the people there and I could call a lot of them my friends. We always came to school early and tried to sneak inside. For many, I think part of this had to do with escaping their abusive home situations. At least at school they knew they would be protected.

Because it was a rather long walk to school, Mark, who used to leave early in the morning for work, would offer me a ride. I came to cherish these moments with him. It was a short ride, but it meant a lot that he would take the time to talk to me. When he dropped me off, he would always ask me if I had any money. He knew that I did not, but he did not want to embarrass me by simply giving it to me. On the other hand, he did not want me to go hungry either. Each day, he would give me a few quarters, or sometimes a dollar and told me to get something to eat for lunch. As I have mentioned, he did not have it to spare, but he always found something to give me. I hope he realizes what this meant to me. I knew what a sacrifice it was for him: that he was probably giving me *his* lunch money and went without eating as a result.

There was a convenience store on the corner near the school and after he drove off, I would go to the store and buy some things and steal others. Most of it was junk food: candy, cupcakes, cookies, etc. There was a candy called "Now & Laters," which are square pieces of flavored taffylike substances. It was one of my favorites and there was an added bonus in that I could share it with my friends when I returned to school. I still see this candy for sale at times and it evokes many memories.

Sneaking into school before classes began was a fun way to start the day. I climbed the drain pipe and lifted open one of the windows to the classroom. Once inside the room, I crept into the hall and ran around to the back entrance and let everyone else inside. From there, a flood of children streaked through the school, running through the halls, laughing and screaming. Most of them got caught, but three of my best friends, Arthur, Marquette, and Jim, sneaked downstairs into the boiler room. This is where the janitors worked/slept. The room was huge and it had many places to hide. It also had old issues of *Playboy* and *Penthouse* magazines.

We sneaked into this room and stole the magazines. Sometimes the janitor was lying on his cot, a half-filled bottle of Southern Comfort whiskey next to him on the floor. These were the most challenging moments, since we had to pass by the cot to get to the locker where the magazines were stored. We thought we were so cool, sneaking past without waking him up, opening his locker, stealing the magazines, and leaving without being seen or heard. Later we repeated the process so he never knew what happened. We took the magazines back to a corner of the boiler room and while we heard the principal and teachers corralling our friends in the halls outside, we learned about anatomy, as well as "turn ons" and "turn offs" of the various models.

While things at school were usually a lot of fun, things at home continued to deteriorate. My father's drinking had not subsided and his abusive behavior increased. As a result, Daryl and I made a point of not being around a lot. When we heard him come in the front door, we usually headed out the back as fast as we could. We ran down the stairs and headed into the backyard of the apartment, jumped the fences into a few neighbors' yards, and were on Howard Avenue in what seemed to be a moment's time. There were instances, however, when I was not so lucky. In those cases, I usually managed to do something wrong and was smacked around for it. This was true even if I was not the one responsible for the problem.

One of my father's favorite head games was to threaten to send me to St. Peter's, a Catholic school right across the street from my inner city public school on Kimberly Avenue. He told me that I would be able to see my friends, but never be able to play with them or to talk to them, because the nuns would never permit it. Now if I had thought about it for a moment, I would have realized that he could never afford to send me to a private school, nor would they want me. But I did not think of that at the time. Instead I saw the only thing I enjoyed being taken away from me. One day he even started to pick up the phone to call the school. The fact that it was eleven at night did not dawn on me.

I flew into a rage and grabbed the phone out of his hand and pushed him away from it. He landed in a sitting position on the couch and bounced right back up at me. My father was not a large man by any means, but to an 11-year-old, he was an imposing figure.

He grabbed me by the throat and lifted me off my feet. He began to scream at me and choke me at the same time. I tried to get away but he was too strong. I kicked with my feet, moved my head, nothing worked. I remember feeling lightheaded, and just as I closed my eyes, Mark came through the door. He grabbed my father and threw him off me. I sank to the floor, dazed. I remember Mark yelling at me to get out of the house, and I stumbled down the front stairs and across the street near his car. I am not sure what happened inside the house, but I heard a lot of yelling and a lot of things breaking. I climbed the fence that surrounded the little league field and ran into one of the dugouts. It was dark out and I figured my father would never be able to find me.

A little later, Mark came out and called my name. I came out and he asked me what had happened. I told him and as we stood near his car talking, my father reappeared. He kept calling me "Mr. Robert" and demanded that I come to him. There was no way I was going to go and I remember Mark saying to me, "Don't let him catch you, Robert. Don't let him catch you." I needed no such advice.

He finally returned to the house but there was no way I was going back there that night. I told Mark I could stay at a friend's house, but in reality it was too late to go knocking on doors. That was a good way to get shot in this neighborhood. I convinced Mark that I would be all right and he left. I ended up sleeping in the dugout that night. The next morning I waited until I saw my father leave and then went into the house.

After changing clothes, washing up a bit, and putting the night's events out of my mind, I went back outside and decided to play some "one-on-one" baseball. This was one of my favorite pastimes. I had never wanted to play little league baseball because I was afraid of getting hit in the head by the pitcher. I had watched all my brothers play as a kid, get hit by pitches, and did not think it was for me. One day I even saw Daryl charge the mound with his bat in his hand after being hit by a pitch: he was something else.

I regretted not playing but I made the most of my time alone. I took a wiffle ball and bat and, mimicking the announcer, introduced the next New York Met to bat. Then I threw the ball into the air and swung. If the ball sailed across the street and hit the fence surrounding the baseball field, it was a triple; over the fence was a homer; and a grounder that hit the curb was an out. I knew all of the Met players: Bud Harrelson, Cleon Jones, Tommy Agee, Ed Kranepool, and I used to play this way all the time. No one could bother me and I knew I was not doing anything illegal.

On this particular day, my mother showed up. I had not heard from her in a long time. On rare occasions, I came home and there would be a pot of stew or something in the refrigerator. I thought Brad or Mark had done something, but later she told me that she was the one responsible. At any rate, Mark must have told her what had happened the night before, because now it was time for me to live with her again.

This led to a number of strange events. Suddenly I moved from New Haven to Hamden, where she had an apartment. Daryl moved in with us and I was sent to Bay Path School. I rode the bus every day and was ostracized by most of the kids and teachers there. They were from working- or lower middle-class backgrounds, which put them light years ahead of me in terms of social standing. They also had benefited from a much more comprehensive educational experience. In short, I was way behind in every phase of life. As I recall, it was during this period that things started to get a little crazy. I moved around a lot. Daryl was too much of a problem for my mother so she sent him back to live with my father, who by this time had moved to Westfield, Massachusetts.

My mother and I lived in a couple of different apartments together, but she was always away, ostensibly working. She worked at a nursing home from 5:30 A.M. to 2:30 P.M. and then went to another part-time job in Chichester, a diner called Lux's. I was on my own a lot during this period, and the television became my most important companion. I spent a lot time alone. Similarly, the living conditions, although a bit cleaner than when with my father, still did not include food and other essentials.

I wanted to stay at Kimberly Avenue School, and when my mother moved us into an apartment in West Haven, a town nearby, I did not want to change schools. This was a hard-fought battle and the only reason I won was my willingness to make sacrifices. I had to get up with her early in the morning so that we would arrive in time for her to start work at 5:30 in the morning. After breakfast was served, she would take me to school and give me money to take the bus home to West Haven. Of course, she was not at home when I arrived, so I was on my own until she came home that evening.

Some nights she did not come home at all. While she said she had to work late or went shopping with her girlfriends, I always knew she was lying. She was having an affair with her boss, a married man with three children of his own. Thus, while she painted the town, I stayed home with no food in the house except several cans of Tab soda, the most disgusting tasting soda since Fresca. I still had to steal to eat.

When we moved back into an apartment in New Haven, I felt as though I could finally deal with the situation. At least I knew where I could scam a sandwich or a meal somewhere. I even went back to the Kimberly Spa and a few of my father's hangouts to see if I could get some food. Unfortunately, my father burned more than a few bridges before he fled to Massachusetts. It seemed like he owed money to everyone on earth and every time they saw me, his friends wanted to know where he was.

I walked the streets at night, hanging out with my friends, getting into trouble. We still lived in a rough section of town, and I knew few people in this neighborhood. Although City Point was only several blocks away, this was an entirely new place with new rules. Being one of the few white guys around, I had to fight a lot. I did not mind this because I was good at it and

I knew this was how the game was played, but some of the fights turned ugly. Kids started pulling knives and other weapons. I had little respect for these kids, thinking to myself that using weapons was a form of cheating. I had learned a long time ago that there was no such thing as a fair fight, however. If I was to survive, I needed to adapt.

I found a paring knife in our kitchen and spent a whole day sharpening it while I watched television. Then I took an old long-sleeved shirt and made a small cut into one of the seams. I slid the knife into the seam and practiced holding my wrist a certain way so that if I simply straightened it out, the knife would slide through the cuff and into my hand. I had seen something like this on the show *The Wild Wild West*. Robert Conrad, who played James West, the coolest fighter I ever saw, had some sort of gadget that slid derringers into his hands at the flick of a wrist. I did not know how it worked but I wanted to try something similar with my knife. Fortunately, I was able to practice enough so that I would not slice my hand open as it slid into my palm. The next time someone started to give me a hard time, I had the knife in my hand before they knew what was happening. It worked! I earned a lot of respect that day.

At one point, my mother started to ask some of her friends if they would be interested in taking care of me. She even offered to pay them (and years later she still had the canceled checks to show me she was a responsible parent). This began the saga of my moving from one home to another, of living with people I did not know.

Follow the Bouncing Ball

It is hard to remember when this all began. There are certainly no records to document the first time my mother pawned me off on to some other family. The only two people who could know are she and I, and I doubt it is something she can or wants to recall. This was a difficult thing for me to understand: if she loved me and wanted to take care of me, then why would she ask friends, acquaintances, and even strangers if they would take me in for a fee? She told me it was because she could not afford to take care of me any longer, but I think this was nonsense. Years later when I was able to access my file from the Department of Child and Families in Connecticut, one social worker who interviewed her asked the same question. In fact, according to the worker's notes, she tried to show my mother that it was more expensive to pay others to do what she could and should be doing. Yet the worker notes that she could not convince my mother otherwise.

At one point, I tried to count the number of families with whom I stayed prior to the State of Connecticut's intervention. Using my age, and the school I attended, I tried to recall which family was responsible for me. While it is a conservative estimate, since I have probably missed a few families over the course of five years time, the number was approximately 13, the unlucky number. Once the state became involved, which I will describe shortly, that number increased to a total of 19.

A lot of people who became involved in my care worked with my mother at the nursing home in New Haven. I would spend a lot of time there, since I had to wait for a ride to school. There were other days that I went with her and stayed the whole day, such as when school was canceled, holidays, vacations, etc. I learned a lot about cooking by watching the employees prepare the meals.

I also learned a lot about hard work. I would help some of them wash dishes, bring back the food carts from the nursing floors, as well as a variety of other tasks. Some of the kids from the Frank Street neighborhood even got jobs there, such as Franky Vollmer, the boy who was intellectually challenged. I got to know most of the nursing and housekeeping staff and spent a lot of time wandering around the halls, the parking lot, and the area surrounding the property. This was a better neighborhood than Frank Street, but not by much. To the north was Yale New Haven Hospital and one of the worst sections of the city: Congress Avenue. I spent a lot of time alone exploring the landscape and trying to keep myself occupied. I would talk to some of the patients, but I was afraid of elderly people, especially sick ones. I would hear their cries and moans at all hours of the day and it made me uncomfortable to be around them.

It was in this environment that my mother sought out guardians who, for a fee of approximately $32 per week, made sure I was fed and had a bed to sleep in. As the following stories indicate, most of these people were more interested in the remunerative rewards than providing me with a safe and stable household. In fact, some of them were downright exploitative, using the money they received, as well as my labor, to their advantage. One might think this is reason enough for the state to intervene. As I will describe later, however, the state was guilty of the same type of negligence. Expediency became the justification for many of the decisions by the social workers, who were supposed to be looking out for what was in my best interest.

Some of the initial families were just as abusive as the home life I left behind at City Point. An example of my mother's lack of insight involved a family that I think suffered from mental disorders. This contact was made through the Recreation Director at the nursing home. Her sister was interested in making some extra money and all of us met at the director's summer home for a weekend in New Hampshire. I learned later that there were two prongs to this attack. First, since the director was on the verge of retiring to her New Hampshire home, if I was amenable to living there, a deal would have been struck to have me stay with them. If not, I would have had an opportunity to live in North Haven with her sister and her family. Parenthetically, I suspect my mother knew this city boy was not going to want to have any part of the New Hampshire situation and would jump at the alternative, which is a suburb of New Haven. As it turned out, this is exactly what happened.

Upon moving in with the family in North Haven, I immediately knew it was a mistake. The family was large, although none of the children or grandchildren lived there. I was told they visited periodically all through the year. In addition to the woman and her husband, the woman's father stayed in a room on the first floor. My introduction to the family was met with a cool reception and the relationship remained unfriendly from the outset. They did nothing to make me feel welcome. Rather, they would go out of their way to remind me what a wonderful thing they had done by taking me in, and that I should be grateful that I had found a compassionate family. When the children and especially the grandchildren visited, it became apparent that a double standard was not only in place and enforced, but encouraged by everyone there. Normally, this could be expected in a situation like this: I was not their biological son, nor was I even related to them. It would have been easy to treat me with respect and dignity, instead of making a show of how insignificant I really was.

I slept in another part of the house from everyone else, and I did not eat the same meals either. While everyone would be eating steak and baked potatoes, my meals consisted of bologna sandwiches and baked beans. For breakfast, while they ate french toast with bacon or ham, I was given small individual boxes of cold cereal. This happened every single day at every single meal. When I protested, I was told I was lucky to be eating anything and if I did not like it, I was free to leave anytime I wanted. I repeatedly complained to my mother about the isolation and the poor treatment and asked to be removed from the household. My mother tried to placate me, telling me that I was getting fed and that the isolation might be something I enjoyed because I was so used to it.

One night I called her from the dining room phone. As I talked to her I leaned against the armrest of one of the dining room chairs. It broke and I was sent crashing to the floor, scraping my side on the jagged edge of the wood. I quickly ended my telephone conversation and went to the bathroom to wash the blood off my shirt. When I returned the woman was screaming at me about how I had wrecked her mahogany wood chair and that I was going to have to pay for it. She rambled on about how irresponsible I was and how "people like me never take care of anything."

At that point I had had enough. I told her off: everything I had been feeling, the way they were treating me, with all the expletives to underscore my points. I told her she would not have to worry about taking care of me anymore, because I would leave right then. Of course, I reminded her that she was legally responsible for me and if anything happened, the police would surely investigate and perhaps it would make the local newspapers. At this point, I left the room and went upstairs. My side was stinging and I was shaking because I was so angry, but I had had enough. I had survived for quite a long time on my own and I would be damned if some snob was going to treat me like garbage and then make me thank her for it. As I was packing my suitcase, she came upstairs and apologized to me. She said she was sorry she lost her temper but that the chair had meant a lot to her and she thought I was simply being careless with her furniture. She said it would be best if we just forgot all about it and let the situation remedy itself. Somehow I did not believe her.

I went to sleep that night wondering how I could get out of this situation. I knew I would not be let off the hook that easily. Just as I fell asleep, around one in the morning, I was being shaken awake. The woman grabbed my hair and literally pulled me into a sitting position. She screamed "You thought this was over? Hah! I'll tell you when it is over! You thought you were going to get away with this, you little prick? Well, think again! Now get your bag packed and call your mother and tell her to come and get you."

My response was simple and I remember this conversation as though it happened yesterday. I said, "Fuck you. You want me out, I'm leaving. But you call her and explain how you treated me like shit. I won't be here when she comes and maybe she'll call the cops on you." With that, I rolled out of bed, grabbed my small suitcase and started putting my clothes in it. When I finished, she was still standing there watching me, hands on hips, toe tapping, the whole bit. I brushed past her, walked downstairs and dialed my mother's number. As it began to ring, I tossed her the phone and ran out of the house. At the time I hoped my mother was home. After all, she had been keeping late hours when I lived with her and now that I was gone, I wondered when/if she eventually came home.

I had no idea where I was going, the only thing I knew was that I would not return to that house. Suddenly I heard the screeching tires of an automobile on the street. A car was speeding toward me. The husband had heard the commotion and raced to bring me back to the house. He stopped next to me and ordered me in the car. Then he yelled at me, to which I responded with a loud expletive.

With that, I continued walking. He pulled the car ahead of me and cut me off. I ran into one of the neighbor's yards and began screaming that he was trying to kill me. I ran up to their front doors and pounded on the storm doors, rang their doorbells, everything I could think of to get their attention. I wanted them to feel some of the humiliation I had endured. A few minutes later, a police cruiser came racing around the corner, lights on and siren blaring. I ran to the cruiser and begged the cop to keep me away from the family. It was terrific. A few minutes later my mother arrived and began to yell at me in front of the police officer.

After about an hour, the situation was resolved and my mother and I left. All the way back to her apartment she kept telling me how she was unable to care for me and that I should stop being such a pain in the neck to all the nice people who were trying to help me. She also said that I was embarrassing her at her place of employment because she had to work with these people. And when I made trouble for them, it reflected poorly on her.

I was less than sympathetic. In fact, I couldn't have cared less about her reputation at work, since it was obvious she cared little about the type of people with whom she placed me. In some cases, she barely knew the person and suddenly found herself asking them if they wanted to take care of her son. The fact that she waved her checkbook around must have convinced her that she was a good mother. What I think she failed to recognize was that this was a choice she was making. She was able to take care of me on her own, but chose her own freedom over her responsibilities as a parent. And the fact that she paid for my care is not especially laudatory; no one was going to do it for free. As I mentioned, she still has these checks to "prove" it many years later.

Whatever the reason, I was suddenly in homes where I did not know the people, I had never met them before, nor could I make a connection to them through someone at the nursing home or one of my mother's friends. A good example of this was a man, I'll call him Ray. He was a bachelor who lived alone in a cottage on a lake about an hour's drive from New Haven. He agreed to take care of me without ever meeting me and told me later that he told my mother "not to worry about the money."

Now this sent alarm bells off in my head, but somehow the significance escaped my mother. This was during the summer when I did not have to worry about school. I figured by the time September came, I would be staying somewhere else anyway. I had been averaging about a few months with each family and it got to the point where I would leave my suitcase packed. Not one person in any of the families ever asked me why I did this, but I figured it was just a matter of time. All of these people had ulterior motives for taking me in, most of them economic.

I suspect they figured they would bring me in and maximize the amount of money they could save by providing me with as little as possible. Added to this was the fact that I was a screwed-up kid with a lot of problems and would not be bullied by anyone. Seeing through their schemes, telling them off, and throwing a few things when the situation turned abusive meant that I did not stay in the good graces of families long.

One day Ray went to the grocery store and I hung around the house. I began nosing around, looking for this guy's angle. I reasoned that nobody takes in a young kid out of the goodness of their hearts, so it was just a matter of time until I figured what this guy wanted. It did not take long. I discovered a number of child pornography magazines and movies in his bedroom closet.

Ray invited my mother and some of his friends to a picnic at his house. She was scheduled to arrive late in the afternoon, so I took some of the magazines, which had his name as a subscriber on the front side of the magazine, with me and hid in the woods until she showed up. When she arrived, I immediately went to her and told her that I needed to leave. She brushed me off and told me I was just being difficult and that I would adjust to the situation.

I showed her the magazines but she would not believe they belonged to him. She contended that there must be some sort of logical explanation. I tried to tell her what was going on but she was unwilling to admit that she made a mistake. She would not take me with her when she left, so I ran away that night. I stayed on the streets for four days in New Haven. I called my mother at work on the fourth day and told her that if she had to resort to begging strangers to take care of me because she was unwilling to do so, I would take care of myself.

I went to my grandfather's house. I felt that this was a viable solution. He was crazy but I felt that, at some level, he cared about me. I had not seen him for a long time, but I was certain he would help me. I went to his house only to discover his car was gone. However, his dog, a black Labrador named Queenie, was tied to the fence near the entrance of the garage. I had seen Queenie when she was a puppy, but looking at her now, I was amazed at how big she had become. To my surprise she recognized me. She licked my face and pawed and rubbed up against me like a long lost friend. Suddenly it began to rain.

My grandfather had built a long "run" or area for Queenie behind the garage. It was a narrow area that ran the length of the yard. Within this long rectangle was a homemade dog house. Queenie and I went in there to get out of the rain. It was quite cramped but it seemed the dog loved to have my company. We laid down together and played with her tennis ball for hours until we both fell asleep. A short while later my grandfather came home. In broken English he asked (I think) what I was doing in the dog house with Queenie. He then laughed as hard and as loud as I had ever seen him.

He brought me inside and made me stay the night. In the morning he made me homemade waffles with an old fashioned waffle iron. It was the first good meal I had in days and I felt safe there. I also felt that for the first time in a long while, I was with someone who cared about me. However, he called my mother and she arrived a few hours later to pick me up. It was the last time I was to ever see my grandfather.

He lived for many years in that house. He also suffered from senility. My brothers and uncles visited him years later and he could not recognize them. I never wanted to see him that way. I wanted to remember my grandfather as the man who used to let me water his lawn and who made me homemade waffles. Perhaps he was crazy, but I like to think that when he was with me, he knew he had the admiration of a small boy.

After I returned to my mother's home, it was not long before she found someone else to take care of me. She was having difficulty finding people who were interested, however. I lived with a young couple for a period of time who had one son and were due to have their second within the year. The husband was 20 years old and the wife 19. They were insecure and had little idea about how to raise a 12-year-old. They did, however, see the benefits of $32 per week and a live-in baby-sitter.

They treated me as though I were an indoor pet. I was not allowed to use the telephone for any reason, I was not allowed to leave the apartment, except to go to school, take out the trash, or to walk to the convenience store for them. I was also responsible for much of the immediate care of the young son. While I admit I learned a great deal about how to change diapers, feed, clothe, and generally raise a child, I am not sure this is what a growing boy should be doing in his spare time.

I was also punished for watching television. The logic behind this was that I should be spending more time helping around the house and with the baby than to enjoy myself watching cartoons. My punishment was to spend time in my room alone, without books, or a radio and I was only allowed to come out of my room to use the bathroom, eat meals, and to help care for the baby as needed. This punishment often lasted for an entire month. I felt like I was given a prison sentence, and I said as much. In fact, I rebelled. I refused to obey anything they said. I left the house at all hours, I stayed late at school, I did anything I could to avoid having to return there.

After several months of this, somehow the state became involved. I am not exactly sure how, but it may have had something to do with the kind of treatment I was receiving here. My mother had also told the state welfare office that she could no longer afford to take care of me and that I needed foster care.

While the state first learned of the McNamara situation in 1969, it was not until 1973 that they officially became involved in my care. Workers informed my mother that having people take care of me without a valid foster care license violated state law. As such, any further decisions concerning my care had to be approved by the state to ensure my best interests were be taken into account. My mother somehow interpreted this to mean that the state wanted to intervene and that she no longer had any responsibilities for my care.

This is something I take up in another chapter, specifically on foster care, but a few other issues should be discussed before moving on to that stage of my life. Issues such as my involvement with gangs, as well as my experiences with racism and poverty. The former is the subject of the next chapter.

References

Klockars, C. (1974). *The professional fence.* New York: The Free Press.

4

Runnin' and Bangin' on the Streets

During those instances when I ran away, I learned quite a bit about street life. Despite the fact that I liked school, there was another type of education I found enjoyable. While growing up on Frank Street in the mid-1960s, I learned a lot about gang life, various forms of vandalism, and watched my older neighbors perfect the art of stealing. Whether it was a bicycle, which would be secretly stored, repainted, and accessorized with parts from other stolen bikes, or shoplifting for food or other items, I had many role models who were willing to talk about their larcenous activities. Looking back now, perhaps I became a field researcher even then, asking them to describe their techniques as well as how they disposed of their ill-gotten booty.

As I grew older and moved to different sections of the city, such as Howard Avenue, when I was about 8 years old, I inevitably became involved in crime, most of which occurred in the context of small groups. While attending Horace Day School with my best friend, Arthur, we learned how to break into the school and ransack the teachers' desk for spare change or other items of value. Sometimes we would try to find the janitors, who, like their counterparts at Kimberly Avenue School, often drank to excess and passed out on cots in the bowels of the boiler room. They were easy marks, but often had little to offer. When we moved to Chichester a year later, where my father worked as a janitor, I found it was easy to have the run of the place after school. On the premise of helping my father clean the classrooms and hallways, I had the opportunity to steal the toys that other students kept in their desks. This was the age of Mattel's Hot Wheels, which were sleek-looking, pocket-sized toy cars with exceptionally good details, such as mag wheels and doors that opened and closed. They even sold plastic race tracks on which the cars could "drag race." While my father cleaned the hallway, I would clean out the desks of several classrooms, sometimes bringing home a dozen or more cars in my pockets. Then I would go to another neighborhood or elementary school and sell them to the kids for less than they would pay at the store. Because the cars were in excellent shape, they would be snapped up with whatever milk money kids were given that day. My cover story was that my family needed the money and I had to sell the cars to help out. This was technically true, but I never intended to give the proceeds to anyone in my family. And the fact that I looked like a kid in dire need of money did not hurt my case either.

After leaving Chichester and returning to New Haven, where I lived with my father above the Kimberly Spa, and attended Kimberly Avenue School, I was introduced by some friends to shoplifting. I had already mastered techniques to steal food, and building off my entrepreneurial skills developed in Chichester, it was a short step to ripping off department stores. A popular fad during this time were wide leather wristbands/ watch holders. These were essentially wide pieces of dyed leather with flaps on the top to hold the watch in place and a small buckle on the bottom to secure it on your wrist. Most kids would tear off the watch straps and simply wear them as a wristband. Sweat bands were also popular. These were simply absorbent pieces of cotton that athletes wore during games. We would steal them, wear them to school, or trade/sell them. In addition to the value of the goods, the thrill of the chase was equally important to us. The excitement generated by going into the store and shoplifting was a thrill that was hard to duplicate.

Years later, Jack Katz [1989] talks about this in his book, *Seductions of Crime*. He argues that there is a sort of seductive appeal to crime, one that somehow magically propels us to commit the act. With regard to shoplifting, or what he calls "sneaky thrills," he accurately captures the essence of what we felt as kids: that the chance of getting caught and outsmarting the store detectives was probably more important to us than to the items we stole. Sometimes we would steal things just to see if we could get away with it.

A kid's status in the neighborhood was based in part on footwear, and Converse All-Stars or Pro Keds were the preferred brands. Obviously we could not afford these luxuries, although I was always amazed to see some of my friends who could. They were just as poor as I was, sometimes worse, yet they were able to acquire top-of-the-line footwear. One solution to this dilemma, which became almost a panacea to my problems, was to simply steal what I needed or wanted. Now stuffing jewelry or a watchband down my pants was one thing: stuffing a pair of shoes is an altogether different proposition. The mission was to come out with a new pair of sneakers without getting caught and with as much creative flair as possible.

I waited until after dinner time, since that was the period when many people came to this store to shop. I walked in and wandered about the store, trying to find the hidden cameras and two-way mirrors behind which many security agents watched for shoplifters. I browsed a bit, lingering in the sporting goods section, where young kids were supposed to hang out, and gradually made my way to the shoe section.

I found a pair of white high-top style Converse All-Stars, complete with the Chuck Taylor signature on the side and made sure they fit properly. This accomplished, I headed to the clothing section and found three pairs of pants and two shirts. I waited until the clerk responsible for checking items in the fitting room was occupied and then slipped behind her into one of the rooms. I pulled the clothes off the hangers and then reattached them in a different way to make it look as though I had tried them on. I then took off my old sneakers and put the new ones on. I hid the shoes under the bench in the fitting room and walked out. I handed the clerk my clothes and said they did not fit properly and continued browsing. I lingered a bit longer and finally headed for the door. By this time I was getting nervous and did my best to keep calm. I saw that Arthur had made it outside and was waiting for me by the mini-carnival rides near the front entrance.

As I started to leave the store the security guard stopped me and asked if the shoes I was wearing belonged to me. I looked up at him and realized I was about to get busted. I gave my best impression of a vanquished opponent and said something like, "Okay, you got me," and relaxed a bit. At that moment I kicked the guard in the shins and bolted toward the electric doors. I was at full speed when the doors started to open. Unfortunately they were moving rather slowly. I hit the door face first and luckily, the door kept moving outward. I ran by Arthur, who knew enough to stay put while the guard chased me through the parking lot. My vision was blurry and I could not see clearly, but I had my Cons and there was no way I was going to let some overweight old man catch me. If he did, I would never hear the end of it.

Later, Arthur said he could have sworn he heard me laughing all the way across the parking lot. I eluded the guard and met up with Arthur later near Washington Park. He had stolen two wristbands and sold them to "a dumb white boy" who paid too much. We spent the rest of the day buying soda and eating Ring Dings, and cupcakes called Yankee Doodles. We met up with some friends and laughed our way through the evening. None of us wanted to leave because the time we shared was much more enjoyable (and safer) than the time we spent with our families.

As a sociologist, most of my time is spent trying to understand and explain phenomena. My own behavior is no exception. Perhaps the most appropriate theories to explain the reasons for my behavior with my friends are found in the work of Edwin Sutherland as well as David Matza and Gresham Sykes.

Differential Association and the Drift Theory

Edwin Sutherland, writing in the late 1930s, stated that any person can be trained to adopt and follow a pattern of criminal behavior. Sutherland explicitly incorporated systematic learning of crime as a central theme in his 1937 case study, *The Professional Thief*. In tracing the criminal career of

"Chic Conwell," Sutherland outlined the social learning process that was said to be essential to a professional thief's understanding of the norms, values, techniques of the criminal trade. In this book, Sutherland likened the learning of crime to the learning of any other "group way of life."

In his statement of the theory, Sutherland proposed that Differential Association was intended as a comprehensive explanation of criminal behavior and is considered applicable to a wide range of noncriminal deviance as well [Sutherland 1947].

Learning deviance involves learning to define certain situations as the appropriate occasions for deviant behavior; to master the techniques of successful deviant activity; and to acquire the motives, drives, attitudes, and rationalizations that justify violation of the norms/laws of a particular society. According to Differential Association, these three things are learned principally in the process of interaction with others, within intimate personal groups [Sutherland 1947].

The crucial step in learning deviance occurs when people acquire an excess of definitions favorable to deviance over definitions unfavorable to deviance. This basically means that the person finds more ways to learn and justify committing deviant acts than he or she does to engaging in conforming behavior. The concept of Differential Association contributed to the idea that deviants were normal people overly exposed to a learning process that equated being normal with what others saw as being deviant. This image of deviance as learned behavior has become one of the most widely accepted modern perspective on deviance.

Drifting into Deviance

Gresham Sykes and David Matza created a modification of Differential Association [1957]. This theory picks up on Sutherland's suggestion that one of the things learned is a set of rationalizations which protects a person against the moral claims of the conventional world. Sykes and Matza's contribution to the learning perspective is also less deterministic than most. It recognizes that deviants live in and often in-between the worlds of conformity and nonconformity.

What Sykes and Matza refer to as "techniques of neutralization" are ways in which deviants are able to separate who they are from what they do. In other words, they can normalize their actions in a variety of ways that allow them to square their self-images to themselves as well as to society. This allows them to "drift" back and forth from conformity to deviance without ever remaining in one category or another, and, at the same time, allows them to continue engaging in deviant or criminal behavior [Sykes & Matza 1957].

As with all theories, there are some problems with the learning perspective. While I will not go into them here, suffice it to say that I believe that much of the reason for my behavior at this point in time had to do with exposure to others who thought criminal behavior was an acceptable path.

Shoplifting was a common activity, but relatively harmless. We also spent a lot of time hanging out, stealing, and playing football or basketball at the various playgrounds around the neighborhood. Most of the big kids left us alone and when we fought, it was usually as a result of a dispute over a touchdown or foul for "hacking" when we tried to make a basket. There were other times when we fought to protect our friends or our reputations, but things were essentially benign. As time passed and we got a little older, the activity took a more serious and violent turn.

Gang Life

Toward the end of the 1960s, and into the 1970s, it became apparent to me that most of my friends were getting involved in more organized types of deviant behavior. We would still hang out together but an increasing amount of their time was spent with another group of kids who were about our age, with several others a bit older. This was my first exposure to gangs.

As more and more of their time was occupied in gang activity, I began to get angry at my friends and confronted them about their loyalty to our group. I also asked them why I was excluded from this new association of friends. We shared food, homework assignments, and fun together, to say nothing of how close we felt to each other by having to endure life in the inner city. There were many nights in which any one of us—Arthur,

Marquette, Kenny, and John—came to each other's homes after a particularly bad encounter with a drunken and abusive parent or relative, in search of food, or simply to relieve the pangs of loneliness that a fractured home life brings. In short, we were close.

It was this type of concern and sensitivity for each other's welfare that prevented them from telling me that I was excluded from the gang to which they belonged because I was white. I had never thought of myself as any different from them in any way, and while my father and a few uncles were clearly racist, I saw my companions as people first, and also as my closest friends.

The gang, the Black Cobras, was made up of only African American members and would not allow "crackers" (whites). In fact, their roaming attacks focused on finding "white boys" who were walking alone on the street. I demanded to meet with the leader of this particular gang. It was a dumb thing to do, but I was young (12 years old), idealistic, and mad as hell. My friends tried to discourage me, saying that it could lead to trouble. I think they were in an uncomfortable position of having to choose between our relationship and the one they wanted from the gang. Nevertheless, I found the gang leader, Leroy, who was all of 17 years old at the time, and considered the "baddest" of all the gang members. I was not intimidated. I told him that these were my friends and that the gang members were just as wrong as the white racists for treating me differently. I had proven myself in several neighborhoods around the city and I was as loyal (or even more so) to my friends as anyone in the gang.

Almost immediately, I was physically attacked by the group of six or seven members present at the time. I was so angry that they would initiate such an attack that I fought with an anger I did not know I possessed. I lost, but I remember thinking that more than a few would remember my name.

Finally, Leroy called a halt to the melee. He picked me up and welcomed me to the gang. He then told me that the initiation ceremony to the Black Cobras was to be "jumped in." I did not realize it but my friends had acted on my behalf and lobbied for my membership in the gang. What was significant about this was that I became the first white in the gang. For a long time after, Leroy jokingly referred to me as the gang's "token nigger." He said that once too often and I privately pulled him aside. We had a brief but intense conversation and those comments were no longer mentioned or used in conversation. I simply reminded him of the fact that of the 15 or so guys who made up the gang, almost a third would support me on this issue and it would damage his reputation. We came to an understanding and became good friends after that.

The thing was, membership into the Black Cobras did not change our behavior all that much. We all stole denim jackets and ripped out the sleeves. Kenny used a black magic marker to draw a picture of a black cobra on the back of each one. He was an extremely talented artist and I still wonder if he ever had a chance to capitalize on his gifts. These were our "colors," to be proudly displayed and protected at all costs.

Other than that, little changed. We still roamed the streets, played football, baseball, or basketball, and generally got into trouble, but nothing really serious. We occasionally stole a car and drove around the city, but it was fairly innocuous stuff by our cultural standards. My first stolen car was a Plymouth Fury, a full-sized vehicle. It was loaded with accessories, such as power steering, air conditioning, and even power windows. About ten of us were walking down Lombard Street when we spotted the car. I "called" it first, which was a sort of territorial marker that gave me the first opportunity to steal it. If I was unsuccessful, then someone else would be given the chance.

To my surprise the door was open and the keys were in the ignition. This was the easiest thing I had ever stolen. Later, when Leroy and some of the other older members of the gang showed me how to "hotwire" a car, they always joked about how I did not need to learn this information since people "gave" me their cars.

At any rate, we drove all around the Hill looking for other friends and enjoying the radio. It must have been an amusing sight to see about eight of us bouncing around in the front and back seats of the car, with me at the wheel, with my head barely above the top of the steering wheel. It was hard to see and work the pedals, but I was not about to ask for help. It was my first stolen car and I was going to enjoy it. We eventually ran out of gas and ditched it. Stealing the car was a lot like most of our activities: it was fun and we really did not mean to hurt anyone. Then something happened.

One of the gang members was found beaten in the bushes of Kimberly Park. Spark, the victim, told us that a group of white kids had found him alone and attacked him. Vowing revenge, Leroy began a maniacal pursuit of the offenders. He scoured the neighborhoods looking for anyone who fit the description given by Spark. Other members of the gang seemed to feed off this need for revenge and began carrying knives and zip guns, which were homemade firearms made of antennas from motor vehicles. Through the use of rubber bands, nails, and bullets, we were able to fashion a semireliable handgun. It was not accurate and reloading was especially problematic, but I think the value of the weapon was found in its menacing features rather than its actual effectiveness. Other members carried baseball bats, sometimes with spikes through the head of the bat, while others used pipes and lengths of chain tied around their waists and secured with a padlock. Instead of a group of guys who hung around together and spent a lot of time engaging in petty crime, we became a gang that made its mark with violence. While we never found the offenders who attacked Spark, our identity changed, as did our approach to life on the streets. Was our gang really a gang? This is a difficult question to answer because, as I mentioned, the term "gang" carries with it many meanings and evokes a number of different images for people.

For some, a gang is a small group of four or five adolescents who loiter on a street corner. For others, the term may identify graffiti artists, drug users, neo-Nazi skinheads, or a group of highly organized youth whose purpose is to generate money from drug dealing. To find some type of working definition of gangs, I need to discuss some of their different characteristics

Gang Diversity

In an effort to address some of the diversity found in the study of gangs, which, in turn, affects how a gang comes to be defined, it is important to describe some of the different types of gangs. Our understanding of gangs in the United States has been colored by sensational accounts of gang activities and of gang life. This image has led many people to believe that gang membership means that violence and involvement in the drug trade is automatic. This is not necessarily the case. While there are indeed a number of gangs involved in drug trafficking (which presents a host of problems for a given community), there are other types of gangs that, although they do not present as serious a threat to social life, raise issues of public concern. While there are several different typologies of gangs, one of the easiest to understand is provided by Richard Cloward and Lloyd Ohlin [1960].

The centerpiece of Cloward and Ohlin's theory is the concept of *Differential Opportunity*. According to this concept, people in all levels of society share the same success goals; however, those in the lower class have limited means by which to achieve them. People who see themselves as failures within conventional society will seek alternative or innovative ways to achieve success. Thus, individuals may become involved in gang life and crime simply because legitimate means of success are unavailable to them.

However, Cloward and Ohlin also see a differential opportunity structure for illegitimate means within society. The significance of this finding is that all opportunities for success, legal and illegal, are closed for most of the youth in inner city environments. Because of differential opportunity, youth are likely to join one of three types of gangs: criminal gangs, conflict gangs, and retreatist gangs [Cloward & Ohlin 1960].

Criminal Gangs

These types of gangs exist in stable, low-income areas where there is a close relationship between adolescents and adult criminals. In these environments, adolescents are recruited into organizations that provide a training ground for a successful criminal career. During this apprenticeship, more experienced members of the gang supervise the new members and limit their activities that might jeopardize the gang's profits. Over time, the new members learn the techniques and attitudes of the criminal world and are introduced to the middlemen of the crime business: fences, pawn shops, drug suppliers, etc.

In perhaps one of the most thorough examinations of this type of gang, Chin [1990] describes the characteristics of Chinese gangs. Chin argues that Chinese gangs are closely associated with, and are controlled by, powerful community organizations. In other words, they are an integral part of community life. These gangs are also influenced, to a great extent, by Chinese secret societies and the norms and values of the Triad subculture. The primary activity of Chinese gangs is making money. Members invest a considerable amount of money in legitimate businesses and development in communities in which adult criminals serve as role models and mentors for gang members.

In keeping with their entrepreneurial efforts, drug use among Chinese gang members is rare. Although involved in drug trafficking, they themselves are not drug users. If a member begins using drugs, he is expelled from the gang. Thus, the establishment of Chinese gangs is not based on illicit drug use or fads. Instead they are intertwined with the economic and social structure of their communities. Additionally, Chinese gangs do not experience the deterioration and poverty that other types of gangs members experience. Rather, Chinese gangs grow and become economically prosperous by maintaining ties with the economic and political structure of their communities. In other words, there is a cultural component to the success of these gangs: they have a certain legitimacy within the community based on the historical experience of the Triad societies [Chin 1990].

Conflict Gangs

Conflict gangs develop in communities identified by their dilapidated conditions and transient populations. There are no "successful" adult criminal role models from whom youths can learn criminal skills. When this occurs, violence is used as a means of gaining status. The conflict gang must be ready to fight to protect their integrity and honor. By doing so, they gain the admiration from their peers and this helps them develop a positive self-image [Klein et al. 1995].

Members of conflict gangs identify their membership with certain colors of clothing. Over the years, many gangs have adopted colors to signify membership. In the case of the Bloods and Crips, the colors are red and blue respectively. These gangs, composed primarily of African Americans, are also territorial and concerned about turf. Members will write their gang name, monikers, names of dead members, or gang slogans on walls, sidewalks, trees, on just about anything that can be seen in public. The Bloods and the Crips have recently focused on the drug trade as a means of financial success, although they, like many African American and Hispanic gangs, derive their status primarily from the use of violence and fighting [Klein et al. 1995; Vigil 1988]. In other words, these gangs attempt to deal with what James Vigil [1988] refers to as their "multiple marginality." In those cases where criminal opportunities do not exist, many have used their proclivity for violence as a status-conferring mechanism.

Retreatist Gangs

Retreatists are those who have attempted to achieve success through both legitimate and illegitimate means. Some may have tried crime or violence but have not been accepted into the conflict or violent gangs, nor do they seem to possess the skills to be included in criminal gangs. Cloward and Ohlin [1960] refer to this group as double failures. They "retreat" into a role on the fringe of society, which usually involves withdrawing from social interaction and the heavy use of drugs.

Vietnamese youth gangs, especially in Southern California, are a good example of this type of gang. Essentially, there are three themes that best characterize Vietnamese gangs: mistrust, hiding, and self-control. While drug dealing in Vietnamese gangs is perceived as too risky and is to be avoided, drug use, especially cocaine, is heavy. Vietnamese gangs maintain their low-profile approach to social life by avoiding conspicuous gang symbols such as tattoos or hand signs. The few that are used as indicators of gang affiliation (such as tattoos) are designed so that they can be easily concealed. In manners of dress, they attempt to blend in to the social landscape to avoid the attention of the police. Finally, the structure of Vietnamese gangs tends to be unorganized and fluid. Membership changes constantly and the rituals and practices of traditional gangs is noticeably absent [Vigil & Yun 1990].

Connections to the Literature

As the research clearly shows, my involvement in the Black Cobras had to do with my affiliations with friends and the need to feel a part of something. This is not to say, however, that once I became a member of the gang I did not partake in their activities or that I felt I could not abide by their rules. In fact, it became immediately apparent that I approached gang life with the same focus I now approach research projects.

This was observed by Spark, who gave me the name "One Speed" as my moniker. I played sports, fought, stole, and approached life with a single-minded determination that can only be described as at full throttle. In Spark's view, I did things all the way or not at all: at one speed. When I last saw him it was years later in a methadone clinic in New Haven, where I was working as a consultant on a Centers for Disease Control and Prevention-sponsored project. Spark was dying of AIDS. Still, he deserves a great deal of credit for having the perceptiveness to understand my nature better than I did at that time. In fact, it has been years since I thought about my life as a gang member and it was the reflections brought on by this project that led me to realize that I have maintained those same traits I possessed as a hard-fighting, quick-handed, and hot-tempered boy.

Gang research also helps to explain the nature of the activities my friends and I engaged in before joining the Black Cobras. Some gang experts might even go so far as to identify what the five of us—Arthur, Marquette, Kenny, Jimmy, and I—experienced in New Haven as a gang. We had no formal name, colors, or other identifying markings, but we felt a sense of responsibility for one another, we used violence and involvement in trouble (see Miller [1958]) as a way of gaining status in our neighborhood, and we gradually got involved in more elaborate forms of crime.

My official time as a member of the Black Cobras ended when I was about 13 and moved to West Haven to live with the Lawrence family (the young couple with children). I was in another town and decided that I needed to start acting in a way that would be easier on my mother. There were no long farewells, no *jumping out* ceremony, no disgrace. I was suddenly gone, and did not return to the area until years later as a researcher at Yale.

A few years later, after I had graduated and began teaching at Furman University, I was given the opportunity to study the nature of gangs with the Police Executive Research Forum. Delving into the recent literature on the subject brought back many memories, some of which were still painful, such as the time Arthur was badly beaten in a gang fight.

As I read through the articles and books documenting the relationship between violence and gangs, I remembered holding his head in my hands as I screamed for someone to call an ambulance. I also remembered how he asked me to promise him that I would not let him die. In reality it was a superficial head wound, but scalp wounds bleed a lot—an awful lot. As I sat there, all I could think about was losing the best friend I ever had because of a stupid rivalry between neighborhoods.

Actually, this had been my first official gang fight. Leroy had an argument with someone in an adjoining neighborhood. The dispute escalated, however, when Leroy found himself surrounded by several of the other person's associates. He managed to escape and called a "war council" meeting. He then sent a message to the other neighborhood kids that the two groups should meet and resolve the problem.

We met in the playground across the street from the Albie Booth Boy's Club, near City Point. Between the interstate and Long Wharf Drive was a basketball court within that small park. Actually, it was not the best location since it was a rather populated area and the police patrolled it with some regularity. We met at dusk one Friday evening. I remember smelling the moisture in the air and thinking it was going to rain. I was nervous and my stomach was cramping and quivering in anticipation of what was about to happen. I watched as my colleagues twirled their weapons nervously or simply stood around, waiting to begin. I too, tried to look cool, but my posturing masked a tremendous fear of the unknown. Although the reasons for the gang fight seem trivial now, at the time they were justifiable and appropriate. I knew I had to show my loyalty and support for a friend and I was not afraid to do that... I just wanted to get on with it.

While many Black Cobras used a variety of weapons, I tended to prefer hand-to-hand combat. When necessary, I brought along pipes and other weapons, but I felt in some ways, it was a form of cheating. To me, the purpose of the fight was to see who was better: a weapon only interfered with the process. I used to tell my friends that I derived a tremendous sense of satisfaction by being able to defeat someone using only my wits and my fists. I said it differently then, of course, but I still feel the same way. Virtually anyone can fire a hail of bullets from a machine gun into a crowd of people. How challenging is that? The fact that 8- and 9-year-olds are now doing it only reinforces this point. This is not to say that gang members cannot fight: rather, I am saying the purpose of fighting, particularly among gangs, has lost much of its meaning.

At any rate, the two groups met and the fight began. The sounds of the fight were different than most other activities: the scraping of feet on the pavement, the sickening sound of metal hitting bone, the grunting and screaming as young men swung their weapons or absorbed a blow. I even heard myself cursing and screaming at my opponents as I fought against them without regard for my safety. As I knocked a freckle-faced African American to his knees, I quickly turned and looked for another attacker, without regard for the injuries I had just inflicted. In that environment, and in those moments, displays of humanity and compassion could get a person killed. It is literally and figuratively an example of Darwin's "survival of the fittest" in its purest form.

As quickly as it began, it ended. It was an intense battle, with many people injured, but suddenly, the court was empty. The only ones left were those who lay unconscious or could not escape on their own. I looked down and realized that I had been injured from a knife or some sharp object. My right arm was bleeding, but not badly. My eye had swollen shut and the knuckles on both hands were a bloody mess. As I looked around, I noticed Arthur lying on the pavement. I quickly ran to him and as spectators gathered to see what had happened, I sat on the ground next to Arthur and held his head in my lap. I thought he was going to bleed to death in my arms. I had heard about cases like this and yelled at the people looking at us to call an ambulance. I was never more angry and afraid than at that moment. As I mentioned, the injury was relatively minor, but at the time, it seemed like Arthur was destined to die.

I still think of my time spent with Arthur and wonder how he is doing. Unfortunately, the odds were stacked against him, as they against were me.

References

Chin, K. (1990). Chinese gangs and extortion. In C. R Huff (Ed.), *Gangs in America* (pp. 129-145). Newbury Park, CA: Sage.

Cloward, R., & Ohlin, L. (1960). *Delinquency and opportunity*. Glencoe, IL: The Free Press.

Katz, J. (1989). *Seductions of crime*. New York: Basic Books.

Klein, M., Maxson, C., & Miller, J. (1995). *The modern gang reader.* Los Angeles: Roxbury.

Miller, W. (1958). Lower class culture as a generating milieu of gang delinquency. *Journal of Social Issues, 14,* 5-19.

Sutherland, E. (1947). *Criminology.* Chicago: The University of Chicago Press.

Sutherland, E. (1937). *The professional thief.* Chicago: The University of Chicago Press.

Sykes, G., & Matza, D. (1957). Techniques of neutralization: A theory of delinquency. *American Sociological Review, 22,* 664- 670.

Vigil, J. D., & Chong Yun, S. (1990). Vietnamese youth gangs in southern California. In C. R. Huff (Ed.) *Gangs in America* (pp. 146-162). Newbury Park, CA: Sage.

Vigil, J. D. (1988). *Barrio gangs: Street life and identity in Southern California.* Austin, TX: The University of Texas Press.

Further Readings on Gangs

Bell, D. (1953). Crime as an American way of life. In M. E. Wolfgang, L. Savitz, & N. Johnston (Eds.), *The sociology of crime and delinquency* (pp. 213-225). New York: John Wiley and Sons.

Black, D. (1983). Crime as social control. *American Sociological Review, 48*, 34-45.

Campbell, A. (1990) Female gangs. In C. R. Huff (Ed.), *Gangs in America* (pp. 163-182). NewburyPark, CA: Sage.

Cohen, A. K. (1955). *Delinquent boys: The culture of the gang.* New York: The Free Press.

Cummings, S. (1995). Anatomy of a wilding gang. In S. Cummings & D. J. Monti (Eds.), *Gangs: The origins and impact of contemporary youth gangs in the United States* (pp. 49-74). New York: SUNY Press.

Fagan, J. (1993). The political economy of drug dealing among urban gangs. In R. C. Davis, A. Lurigio, & D. Rosenbaum (Eds.) *Drugs and community* (pp. 137-149). Chicago: University of Chicago Press.

Fagan, J., & Chin, K. (1991). Social processes of initiation into crack use and dealing. *Journal of Drug Issues, 21*, 313-343.

Fagan, J. (1990). Social processes of delinquency and drug use among urban gangs. In C. R. Huff (Ed.), *Gangs in America* (pp. 129-145). Newbury Park, CA: Sage.

Feyerherm, W., Pope, C., & Lovell, R. (1993). *Gang prevention through targeted outreach.* Washington, DC: Office of Juvenile Justice and Delinquency Prevention.

Hagedorn, J. (1988). *People and folks: Gangs, crime and the underclass in a rustbelt city.* Chicago, IL: Lakeview Press.

Horowitz, R. (1983). *Honor and the American dream: Culture and identity in a Chicano community.* New Brunswick, NJ: Rutgers University Press.

Huff, C. R. (1989). Gangs, organized crime, and drug-related violence in Ohio. In *Understanding the enemy: An informational overview of substance abuse in Ohio.* Columbus, OH: Governor's Office of Criminal Justice Services.

Huff, C. R. (Ed.). (1990). *Gangs in America.* Newbury Park, CA: Sage.

Jankowski, M. (1991). *Islands in the street: Gangs and American urban society.* Berkeley, CA: University of California Press.

Joe, D., & Robinson, N. (1980). Chinatown's immigrant gangs. *Criminology, 18,* 337-345.

Joe, K. (1994). Myths and realities of Asian gangs on the west coast. *Humanity and Society, 18*(2), 3-18.

Kenney, D. K., & Finckenauer, J. O. (1995). *Organized crime in America.* Belmont, CA: Wadsworth.

Maxson, C., & Klein, M. (1990). Street gang violence: Twice as great or half as great. In C. R. Huff (Ed.), *Gangs in America* (pp. 71-102). Newbury Park, CA: Sage.

Maxson, C., & Klein, M. (1989). Street gang violence. In N. A. Weiner & M. E. Wolfgang (Eds.), *Violent crime, violent criminals* (pp. 198-234). Newbury Park, CA: Sage.

Miller, W. (1990). Why the United States has failed to solve its youth gang problem. In C. R. Huff (Ed.), *Gangs in America* (pp. 263-287). Newbury Park, CA: Sage.

Miller, W. (1975). *Violence by youth gangs and youth groups as a crime problem in major American cities.* National Institute for Juvenile Justice and Delinquency Prevention. Office of Juvenile Justice and Delinquency Prevention. Washington, DC: U.S. Department of Justice.

Padilla, F. (1992). *The gang as an American enterprise.* New Brunswick, NJ: Rutgers University Press.

Sanders, W. (1994). *Gangbangs and drive-bys: Grounded culture and juvenile gang violence.* New York: Aldine de Gruyter.

Shaw, C. R. (1930). *The jack-roller: A delinquent boy's own story.* Chicago, IL: University of Chicago Press.

Shaw, C. R., & McKay, H. D. (1942). *Juvenile delinquency and urban areas.* Chicago, IL: University of Chicago Press.

Short, J. F., Jr. (1990). Cities, gangs, and delinquency. *Sociological Forum, 5,* 657-668.

Short, J. F., Jr., & Strodtbeck, F. (1965). *Group processes and gang delinquency.* Chicago, IL: University of Chicago Press.

Spergel, I. (1990). Youth gangs: Continuity and change. In N. Morris & M. Tonry (Eds.), *Crime and justice: An annual review of research,* Vol. 12. Chicago, IL: University of Chicago Press.

Takagi, P., & Platt, T. (1978). Behind the gilded ghetto. *Crime and Social Justice, 9*(2), 2-25.

Thraser, F. M. (1927). *The gang: A study of 1,313 gangs in Chicago.* Chicago, IL: University of Chicago Press.

Traub, S. H., & Little, C. B. (1985). *Theories of deviance.* Itasca, IL: F.E. Peacock Publishers.

U.S. General Accounting Office. (1989). *Nontraditional organized crime: Law enforcement officials' perspectives on five criminal groups.* Washington, DC: U.S. Government Printing Office.

Wooden, W. S. (1995). *Renegade kids, suburban outlaws.* Belmont, CA: Wadsworth.

Yablonsky, L. (1959). The gang as a near group. *Social Problems, 7,* 108-117.

5
They Called Me Oreo: Race in the Inner City

As I mentioned, my time spent in New Haven was, among other things, a cultural experience that I have never forgotten. While the city was full of racial tensions and many families tried to pass along their racist ideologies from one generation to another, I was fortunate enough to somehow know that it was wrong. My family, particularly my father and his brothers, preached racial disharmony and tried to feel superior to our African American neighbors. However, I never felt we were in any better position than they were.

I was fortunate because few of my friends ever thought of me as a "cracker." I was one of them: a person who lived in the same neighborhood, attended the same school, and suffered from the same type of social and economic adversity. More important, I had earned their respect. There was no privilege according to birthright on these streets. The only respect you received was what you earned. This involved bravery, courage in the face of danger, street savvy in dealing with others, and a sense of loyalty to your comrades. It did not matter that I was white. To me, what mattered was what I stood for. It is ironic to look back on those days in which the racists were our parents, uncles, or the occasional bully in the neighborhood. A bunch of kids less than 14 years old knew more about racial harmony, fairness, and equality than most people who determine public policy.

This is not to say we did not fight among each other. It is to say, rather, that the fights were based on behavior not on race or ethnicity. When we would joke around and call each other "nigger," I had come to accept the designation without thinking about it: I was one of them. Few white people could walk into a predominantly black neighborhood in New Haven in the late 1960s and early 1970s and call an African American kid by that name: I could and had. Because of the overwhelming number of African Americans in my neighborhood, at times my friends would jokingly call me Oreo, after the cookie, which represented my status as a white person being surrounded by people of color.

In many ways, I had suffered the same kinds of problems in dealing with people that my friends had. Now, some skeptics might be thinking this was impossible because I could not hide the fact that I was white. Many experts on race and ethnicity would argue that in these situations, where I would be dealing with racists, I would be given preferential treatment or opportunities that my friends, as African Americans or Hispanics, would not be given (see Feagin and Vera [1995]; Ravitch [1990]; Swinton [1990]; and Massey and Denton [1993]). While this may be true, and there were some instances when I was treated differently, such as my run-ins with the police and teachers, I do not believe I was treated substantially different for three main reasons. First, while there was still a large Italian population in New Haven, there was also an increasing Puerto Rican population. While I am half Italian and half Irish, there have been several instances, even relatively recently, when I have been mistaken for a Hispanic man. As an example, several years ago my wife and I went to a deli in the Wooster Street area. This particular place, like most of the establishments in the area, was owned and operated by an Italian family. I had come to know the owners by their first names and they had known me by mine. One day, one of the owners asked me if I was a Latino. If I can be mistaken for a Hispanic by an Italian man who has lived in New Haven for decades, it is not unbelievable that I could be mistaken for and treated like a minority by others.

The second reason had more to do with my reaction to preferential treatment. Recall that I was fiercely loyal to my friends in the neighborhood and would always try to include them in whatever deal or opportunity that arose. For example, one day a grocery store clerk who knew my mother offered me a submarine sandwich because he knew we were so poor. I asked him to slice it into several pieces so I could share it with my friends. When the man realized that my "friends" were not good Italian boys, but rather a bunch of, as he put it, "nigger hoodlums," he refused. He said the sandwich was for me, not for them. As a result, I refused the sandwich completely, although I was hungry at the time. I cannot offer an explanation for my behavior that day (and other days like it) except to say that I knew it was wrong. I somehow felt that it was better to go hungry than to betray my friends. I could not accept the fact that a racist was going to give me something that others equally deserved. I remember that day almost as vividly as the day it occurred: I was incensed at the man for putting me in that position. To me, these were my friends and we were all hungry. It did not matter that this grocer had the "hots" for my mother, the right thing to do was to feed the kids. He thought enough of me to make sure I was okay, why not include others like me?

Finally, I believe that I experienced almost as much discrimination and prejudice as my African American friends, largely because a great deal of the unfair treatment was based on social class, not race. We were poor and no one wanted to give us anything. I remember teachers recoiling in fear as they checked our clothes for bugs and our heads for lice. For the most part, they wanted nothing to do with us. Other people acted in a similar manner. Their reactions to us were based on the fact that we were dirty, poor, and malnourished kids, not necessarily because we were black or white. Did my friends get stigmatized and discriminated against? Absolutely. Did I feel the pains of racism and discrimination? Without a doubt.

Did I know what it was to be a minority? Although it does not fit exactly into the sociological definitions of what constitutes a minority group, I think I know what it felt like to be singled out and different. Most of the sociological definitions of minority groups describe them as "a group of people who are singled out from others for differential and unequal treatment, and who also regard themselves as objects of collective discrimination" [Dworkin & Dworkin 1982, p. 32] (see Wirth [1945]; Stone [1985]; and Dworkin and Dworkin [1982]). Was I a minority according to this definition? The answer seems obvious. Size of the group is not necessarily what defines a minority group, status does. One can be a member of a group that constitutes a numerical majority and still be considered a minority. A good example was the Apartheid system in South Africa. Thus, being a minority is a social status, one that is defined by the standing to other, more powerful groups in a society.

Some scholars use race and ethnicity as the defining characteristic, while many contemporary scholars use variables such as gender, religion, age, sexual preference, the poor, or even the physically challenged (see Sagarin [1971]; Makielski [1973]; and Levin and Levin [1982]). The common denominator in these distinctions is clearly tied to their access and use of power: those who do not have it are considered minorities. In this way, I do believe I was singled out for unfair treatment, but it was based on my social class, not on my race. In sum, I think I know what it was like to be different.

When I talk to people of color who feel as though they have been oppressed, I sometimes learn that they are middle- to upper middle-class African Americans. I do not mean to trivialize the issues of racism, prejudice, and discrimination, nor do I mean to suggest that all middle-class African Americans act this way, or even that these situations occur frequently. When they do, however, I often take exception to their comments that imply they are oppressed and, as a white man, I am somehow responsible for their situation. It is during these types of conversations that I wonder what they actually know about being oppressed. Many have gone to better schools, have had more opportunities, and generally had a life much more privileged than I, but they tell me they are exploited and I am somehow responsible. This simply does not make sense. While I may not sound politically correct, these people are taking advantage of the political and social climate, which is currently trying to rectify some of the atrocities of our past. To me, they cheapen the efforts of such brave men as Martin Luther King, Jr., Jesse Jackson, and Nelson Mandela.

When dealing with the issue of race, it is almost impossible to avoid the problems associated with poverty. In fact, in many cases the two go hand in hand. But what do we really know? Where are we in terms of understanding the problems associated with race and poverty? After discussing the issue of race and poverty, allow me to offer a few thoughts that may shed light on why the problem persists and deli clerks (and others) still refuse to help hungry children.

The Poverty Debate: Culture vs. Structure

In the 1960s, Daniel Patrick Moynihan [1965] and Oscar Lewis [1966] were leading proponents of the "culture of poverty" theory. Moynihan explains the behavior of many African Americans by asserting this community has a distinct culture with its own value systems.

Similarly, in his study of Latino families, Lewis [1966] acknowledges structural factors like unemployment, social, economic, and educational isolation as being deleterious on the poor; however, these structural elements only explain how people initially become poor [Flanagan 1995]. Lewis proposes that poor children are socialized into a value system that keeps them from becoming hard working and productive members of society [Jencks & Peterson 1991; Wilson 1987].

In his description of the culture of poverty, Lewis argues that in an attempt to adapt to the environment, a series of values emerge that become internalized and are passed from one generation to the next. He contends that these values and attitudes reinforce behaviors that keep one in poverty. This implies that changes in social policy or other types of programs will not work, because the rewards of poverty-related behavior within the culture are perceived as greater than the rewards for engaging in mainstream behavior.

This view of poverty focuses on the interconnection between cultural traditions, family history, and individual character. Specific cultural traits emerge from being poor, and would still influence people's behavior even if they were offered opportunities to improve their situation (see White [1995]).

Associated with the culture of poverty is a related perspective that asserts welfare actually creates poverty. Charles Murray [1984] claims that the poor do not see the value in caring for themselves, because they know that the state will do it for them. According to this view, poor people choose their lifestyle because doing otherwise would require working hard and meeting one's societal obligations [White 1995].

Murray argues that every individual is responsible for improving his or her own position in life and as such, we cannot hold the government responsible for making these changes for them. Murray is clearly stating that people are poor simply because they are either lazy and/or do not possess any type of work ethic.

In support of these contentions, Murray and others often point to the purchasing practices of some poor families [Gans 1993; Gilbert & Kahl 1987; Sidel 1986]. They argue that poor people own too many leisure items like expensive clothes, stereo equipment, televisions, and luxury automobiles. Those who buy these types of things are considered wasteful and too present-oriented, and therefore uninterested in changing their current status. Those who only buy the basic necessities are characterized as committed to changing their poverty status because they "appreciate the value of the dollar" [White 1995].

What is interesting about this evaluation of the poor is that it does not account for the fact that we are clearly a materialistic society. We are so insecure that we feel we must flaunt our affluence through status symbols and what Thorsten Veblen [1950] referred to as "conspicuous consumption." Another way of looking at this then, is to say that the poor, like the rich, are simply trying to attain part of the "American dream" through what they own. As such, they are also subscribing to mainstream societal values.

The Structuralist Approach

Structuralists argue that the poor have the same aspirations and desires as everyone else. The difference is that they have few opportunities to climb the ladder of success. In other words, they want the American dream as much as the next person, but are unable to attain it. The problem is that the barriers in place that prohibit their success are intertwined with elements in the social structure (see Hayward, Grady, and Billy [1992]).

As White [1995] describes, there are essentially three approaches used in Structuralist accounts of poverty [Aponte 1991; Jencks & Peterson 1991; Santiago & Wilder 1991; Zinn 1989]. In the *mismatch hypothesis*, shifts in the location of manufacturing has resulted in the isolation of minorities in urban areas. That is, this population is removed from the kinds of employment they normally seek because the jobs simply do not exist in those areas any longer. Additionally, with what has become known as "white flight" or the movement of middle-class and some lower class populations out of the inner city, there are fewer tax revenues from which the city can draw to provide needed services (see White [1995]).

The second model focuses on *labor market segmentation*. This explanation suggests that the racial distribution of jobs is unbalanced. African Americans and Hispanics are more likely to be in positions requiring manual labor [White 1995]. This secondary labor market is largely unstable, so people who occupy it are paid less and have few opportunities for advancement (See Jencks and Peterson [1991]).

Third, some critics have argued that lower quality schools are often found in low-income communities, because the public school system is based on property taxes from the community (see, for instance, Kozol [1991]). As a result, schools in these communities have problems competing with private schools and suburban public schools for teachers, equipment, and other important resources (see Gans [1993]). The upshot of this is that the children are less likely to be prepared for college.

Additionally, Structuralists have argued that Culturalists are responding to the small fraction of people who chose to be out of work. Most poor people retain the same values that are identified with the middle class, but what is different is that they do not have the same mechanisms with which to realize their goals (see White [1995] and Anderson [1991]).

For them, the solution to persistent poverty lies in the *system*, not the individual. Consequently, social policy that addresses racial discrimination, inequality, and stratification is the only way poverty can be alleviated. African American and Hispanics who are poor are subjected to inordinately challenging oppression because of the way race operates within the social structures of the United States.

Finally, there are those social scientists and policy analysts who think that the Great Society and other progressive measures geared toward the poor has resulted in the loss of American culture [White 1995[. In this view, multicultural reform, bilingual education, and other initiatives are not making the poor "more equal." Rather, these efforts fragment American society into a set of individual groups rather than unifying them.

In a similar way, critics such as Steele and Wilkins [1993] argue that programs like affirmative action simply exacerbate the problem by focusing on racial inequality and result in tensions between the races. Roger Wilkins [1993] sees poverty and race as interconnected. As such, they both must be redressed for poor people of color to survive poverty. This means that for solutions to be effective, we must confront the structural influences on poverty, while at the same time realize the unique ways that race affects how poverty is experienced [White 1995].

What Does All This Tell Us?

The issues surrounding race and poverty, namely policy decisions like affirmative action and welfare reform, are far from clear. With regard to programs like affirmative action, many conservatives, such as Governor Pete Wilson of California, argue that the issue should be based on merit, not on race or other factors. This has a certain appeal to most people. After all, it is based on the idea that has a ring of authenticity to it: fairness. If the person is the most qualified for the job, then she or he should be the one hired. What could be more American than that?

Wilson and other conservatives are also quick to point out that the increase in the number of middle-class African Americans are indicators that we no longer need "set aside" programs for businesses and we no longer need strategies such as affirmative action, because they have accomplished what they were intended to do: to give people of color and other minorities the opportunities to gain a foothold in the labor market.

When I have discussed the problems of the poor with others, especially my family, it seems obvious that there are a number of flaws to the merit-based argument, perhaps the most glaring of these, are ones involving logic. As I try to explain to them, the only reason some minorities, in this case, African Americans, have been able to make the strides of success are *because* of programs such as affirmative action. While the conservatives argue that we have achieved equality, they fail to recognize that it was forced upon them: they would not have done so willingly. And this, it seems to me, is the crux of the issue.

We all know that people are given jobs because of who they know, are related to, or for some reason other than merit. And for a long time, many white men have had the upper hand in determining to whom the job was given. With the passage of legislation which took away that discretion and authority and with the jobs going to unknown minorities instead of friends, relatives, or college mates, suddenly the issue becomes one of merit. Do minorities get jobs for which they are unqualified? Sometimes, but so does the boss's son who is put into an executive position when he knows little about the business. And there are countless other examples where unqualified people get the job over a qualified applicant simply because they know someone in the company. The issue of merit is not the reason for the concern.

The real issue is one of power. Some people who have had it for a long time are suddenly finding they are losing it. We cannot escape this fact. People will never be exactly equal and our history shows us that we will never simply "do the right thing" when it comes to including minorities in the work force. This was the reason legislation was enacted in the first place. If we are truly interested in equality and fairness, we should have quotas to include an equal proportion of every race, ethnicity, and gender in the job market. But we are not. We are interested in helping ourselves, our friends, and people we like—people who are similar to us. As such, we will never be able to achieve equality unless we make it a priority. And as I mentioned, since this is really not the issue anyway, the conservatives will never accept such an alternative.

A second and related point can also be made. If we as a society are honestly interested in giving minorities a legitimate chance to become qualified candidates, why have we continued to perpetuate the class distinctions in education? The sociological literature on the relationship between education, income, and occupation is well known, especially concerning life chances of parents and their ability to pass those opportunities on to their children. (See for instance Blau and Duncan [1967]; Sewell, Haller, and Ohlendorf [1970]; Hout and Morgan [1975]; Alexander, Eckland, and Griffin [1975]; Jencks and Peterson [1979]; Krymkowski [1991]; and England [1992].) Those who are able to obtain a good education can expect many lucrative career opportunities, and the same is true in reverse. Those with substandard educations will likely occupy jobs in the lowest paying sectors of the market.

Since minorities are usually found at the lower end of the educational continuum, how will they ever be given a chance to compete on an equal footing? If we abolish programs that require employers to give minorities a chance to become a part of the system, how will they do it on their own?

The only viable way will be to somehow acquire the same or similar educations. Yet, there are clear differences in the amount of money spent in education between social classes. Moreover, these are the programs that have been attacked by the conservatives during the latest sweep of budget cuts. What this does is to make it even more difficult for minorities to compete, which in turn, will shunt them out of the job market since someone else will almost always be "more qualified."

Again, this is not about merit. We can all agree that the most qualified person should get the job. What has happened, however, is that we have made it nearly impossible for minorities and the poor to obtain the necessary credentials to compete. The end result is the same: few minorities get the jobs. In this carefully constructed argument, however, the focus will not be on unfair treatment, rather the argument will be that there are no qualified minorities to do the job—of course not. It is a sophisticated and shrewd strategy that is much more likely to be accepted at face value. People who promote this line of thinking have learned something from our history of race relations: minorities and others will now take exception to blatant forms of racism and discrimination. If they appeal to reason and logic, however, even if it is contrived, they may still be able to get what they want.

If we wanted to give minorities an honest chance to compete without programs like affirmative action, we would have to spend a great deal more on education and other programs targeting minorities than we would spend on affluent children. This is necessary simply because so many poor children are behind in virtually all phases of learning. How likely is it that affluent parents are going to be willing to pay more taxes to give minorities a chance to compete? Rather, they will contend that their children should benefit from their resources, not minority children.

In sum, we seem to want it both ways. We say we want equality, but what that really means is we want equality for us, not for everyone else. We will provide advantages for our children but not others; we will help our children to achieve social mobility, but we resent it when we are forced to give those same opportunities to others. We say the basis should be merit, but what we are really saying is that we do not want the choice taken out of our hands. We say everyone should be on an equal footing, but our behavior and social policies continue to perpetuate the same type of discrimination that has existed for centuries. And we sit in wonder when riots occur and minorities react out of frustration. What would most people do in that situation?

References

Alexander, K. L., Eckland, B. K., & Griffin, L. J. (1975). The Wisconsin model of socioeconomic achievement: A replication. *American Journal of Sociology, 81,* 324-342.

Anderson, E. (1991). *Streetwise.* Chicago, IL: University of Chicago Press.

Aponte, R. (1991). Urban Hispanic poverty: Disaggregations and explanations. *Social Problems, 38*(4), 516-528.

Blau, P. M., & Duncan, O. D. (1967). *The American occupational structure.* New York: John Wiley.

Dworkin, A. G., & Dworkin, R. J. (Eds.). (1982). *The minority report: An introduction to racial, ethnic and gender relations.* New York: Holt, Rinehart, and Winston.

England, P. (1992). From status attainment to segregation and devaluation. *Contemporary Sociology, 21,* 643-647.

Feagin, J. R., & Vera, H. (1995). *White racism.* New York: Routledge.

Flanagan, W. B. (1995). *Urban sociology: Images and structure.* Needham Heights, MA: Allyn and Bacon.

Gans, H. J. (1993). *People, plans, and policies.* New York: Columbia University Press.

Gilbert, D., & Kahl, J. A. (1987). *The new American class structure.* Chicago: The Dorsey Press.

Hayward, M. D., Grady, W. R., & Billy, J. O. G. (1992). The influence of socioeconomic status on adolescent pregnancy. *Social Science Quarterly, 73*(4), 750-72.

Hout, M., & Morgan, W. R. (1975). Race and sex variations in the causes of the expected attainments of high school seniors. *American Journal of Sociology, 81,* 364-394.

Jencks, C., & Peterson, P. E. (1991). *The urban underclass.* Washington, DC: Brookings Institution.

Kozol, J. (1991). *Savage inequalities.* New York: Crown.

Krymkowski, D. H. (1991). The process of status attainment in Poland, the U.S. and West Germany. *American Sociological Review, 56,* 46-59.

Lewis, O. (1966). *La vida: A Puerto Rican family in the culture of poverty.* New York: Random House.

Levin, J., & Levin, W. (1982). *The functions of discrimination and prejudice.* New York: Harper and Row.

Makielski, S. J. (1973). *Beleagured minorities.* San Francisco: W.H. Freeman.

Massey, D. S., & Denton, N. A. (1993). *American apartheid.* Cambridge, MA: Harvard University Press.

Moynihan, D. P. (1965). *The negro family: The case for national action.* Washington, DC: Office of Policy Planning and Research, U.S. Department of Labor.

Murray, C. (1984). *Losing ground: American social policy 1950-1980.* New York: Basic Books.

Ravitch, D. (1990). Multiculturalism: E pluribus plures. *The American Scholar, 59*(3).

Sagarin, E. (Ed.). (1971). *The other minorities.* Waltham, MA: Ginn.

Santiago, A. M., & Wilder, M. G. (1991). Residential segregation and links to minority poverty: The case of Latinos in the United States. *Social Problems, 38*(4), 492-515.

Sewell, W. H., Haller, A. O., & Ohlendorf, G. W. (1970). The educational and early occupational attainment process: Replication and revisions. *American Sociological Review, 35,* 1014-1027.

Sidel, R. (1986). *Women and children last.* New York: Penguin Books.

Stone, J. (1985). *Racial conflict in contemporary society.* Cambridge, MA: Harvard University Press.

Steele, S., & Wilkins, R. (January/February 1993). Backtalk. *Mother Jones, 17.*

Swinton, D. H. 1990. Economic progress for black Americans in the post-civil rights era. In G. E. Thomas (Ed.) *U.S. race relations in the 1980s and 1990s.* New York: Hemisphere Publishing.

Veblen, T. (1950). *Theory of the leisure class.* Chicago: University of Chicago Press.

White, R. (1995). Race and poverty: An urban reality? In K. M. McNamara & R. P. McNamara (Eds.), *The urban landscape: Selected readings* (pp. 149-178). Landham, MD: University Press of America.

Wilson, W. J. (1987). *The truly disadvantaged.* Chicago, IL: University of Chicago Press.

Wirth, L. (1945). The problem of minority groups. In P. I. Rose (Ed.), *Nation of nations: The ethnic experience and the racial crisis* (pp. 137-163). New York: Random House.

Zinn, M. B. (1989). Family, race, and poverty in the eighties. *Signs, 14*(4), 856-874.

Further Readings on Race and Poverty

Farley, J. E. (1995). *Majority-minority relations.* Englewood Cliffs, NJ: Prentice-Hall.

Frazier, F. (1957). *Black bourgeoise: The rise of a new middle class.* New York: The Free Press.

Jaret, C. (1995). *Contemporary racial and ethnic relations.* New York: Harper Collins.

Jencks, C. (1992). *Rethinking social policy: Race, poverty, and the underclass.* Cambridge, MA: Harvard University Press.

Jencks, C. (1979). *Who gets ahead: The determinants of the effect of family and schooling in America.* New York: Basic Books.

Jiobu, R. M. (1990). *Ethnicity and inequality.* New York: SUNY Press.

Kivisto, P. (1995). *Americans all.* Belmont, CA: Wadsworth.

Marger, M. N. (1994). *Race and ethnic relations* (3rd ed.). Belmont, CA: Wadsworth.

Parillo, V. N. (1980). *Strangers to these shores.* New York: Macmillan.

Schaefer, R. T. (1993). *Racial and ethnic groups.* New York: Harper Collins.

U.S. Bureau of the Census. (1994). *Statistical Abstract of the United States.* Washington, DC: Author.

U.S. Bureau of the Census. (1993). *Statistical Abstract of the United States.* Washington, DC: Author.

U.S. Bureau of the Census. (1990). *Statistical Abstract of the United States.* Washington, DC: Author.

Wilson, W. J. (1978). *The declining significance of race.* Chicago, IL: University of Chicago Press.

6

Neglect, Abuse, and State Intervention

The situation with the Lawrence family, where I was confined to the apartment and spent a lot of time raising two children, deteriorated rapidly after a short time. At this point, the State of Connecticut intervened. It was explained to me that what my mother was doing was illegal. It was unlawful for a person to pay another for the total and complete care of a nonrelative minor without being licensed by the state as a certified foster parent. My mother was unaware of this, as were all the people she had been paying at that point. And if they did know, or knew they would never be licensed, they remained silent since they were not about to sacrifice an easy $130 every month.

The state interviewed the Lawrence family and determined they were unacceptable foster parents for me. The problem then became finding a licensed family that was interested in dealing with a 12-year-old troublemaker. To be honest, I had tried hard not to cause any trouble during this time. In some way, I thought that I might be causing the problem with all these families, so I decided to give compromise a try. I will admit I was skeptical, thinking that the reason the other situations did not work out had more to do with my unwillingness to be exploited than anything else. When I did not kowtow to these people and act as though they had saved my life, they did not like it much. This was especially true when I told them they were being well-paid for their efforts. At times I even mentioned that I thought they actually worked for my mother: that went over *real* well.

After a long talk with my mother, I decided that I would give the families an honest chance and rely on her to select a better caliber of people. Besides, the state was now involved, so even if my mother continued to make convenience the important factor in finding a place for me to stay, surely the state would never allow her to place me with them. That was my mistake. I quickly learned that the state had their own problems in handling children. It seemed that some of the social workers who became involved in my case would express outrage at the unfair way I had been treated, only to demonstrate their own level of incompetence and/or lack of understanding of the issues. Everyone knew what was wrong and everyone seemed to know exactly what had to be done. Yet no one ever bothered to ask me what I wanted. Perhaps it was due to the difficulty of placing teenagers in foster care (a difficult task at best). This does not justify the atrocious lack of professionalism and willingness to sacrifice my welfare to clear a caseload, however. Were all my social workers incompetent? I can only say that while they may have had the best of intentions, they did little more than exacerbate the problem and continued to compound the error by failing to identify the core issues related to my care.

In sum, when the state intervened in my case, they informed my mother that she would still be required to continue paying for my care, but they felt they were in a better position to select foster families. As I mentioned, I now know that my situation is a common one for foster children.

Modern Foster Care

As far back as the late 1950s, the research on foster care began to call attention to serious problems in the system in this country. (See for example, Mass [1969]; Fanshel and Shinn [1978]; Wald [1976]; Gruber [1978]; Shyne and Schroeder [1978].) During the 1970s, the number of children in foster care began to increase dramatically, with an estimated 500,000 children from 1975-1977 [Pelton 1978; Knitzer et al. 1978]. Children were put mainly in foster homes, but also in institutions, group homes, and other places by welfare agencies or were placed under the authority of other public agencies such as the juvenile justice system, mental health agencies, and special education. The number of children in these categories was estimated to be another 250,000 [Knitzer et al. 1978].

The concern over the number of children in foster care—as well as the outcry by many health care professionals that children stayed in the system too long and were moved around too much—led to what was known as "permanency planning" during the mid to late 1970s. This strategy later became a significant component of the Adoption Assistance and Child Welfare Act of 1980. Basically, many child welfare workers believed that children were being harassed by a system in which they stayed indefinitely and drifted from one home to another, and had less than adequate supervision of their cases. The main thrust of the permanency planning movement was aimed at children already in foster care: to either get them returned to their natural parents or, if that option is not available, to allow them to be adopted. Other options included legal guardianship and planned long-term foster care.

According to the National Foster Parent Association, in 1995 the number of children in licensed foster care in the United States was 520,000 (this does not include children in unlicensed homes), and the number of licensed foster homes was approximately 125,000. Further, Charles Black, Director of the Association, states that the number of children entering foster care is increasing, while the number of licensed homes is dwindling.

There is also the problem of obtaining an accurate assessment of the size of the population. While some states have computerized their files, which makes access to this type of information easier, many have not. And even those states that have the technology, many are unable to retrieve information beyond a ten- or 12-year period. While foster care has been regarded as a temporary living arrangement for children until their parents are able to adequately care for them, the fact is that many children have stayed in foster care for many years. Fanshel and Shinn [1978] for instance, in their study of 624 New York City children who entered foster care at the age of 12 years or younger, and who had remained at least 90 days, found that 36% were still in foster care five years later. Additionally, half of the children who were under 2 years old when they entered foster care were still there after five years, almost half of whom were African American. Similarly, Mass [1969] found that of children who were in foster care at least three months, 31% were still in the system after ten years.

As of 1980, of the estimated 40,000 children in foster care in New York State, the average length of time in the system was 4.4 years, with 14% participating for ten years or more. There are several other studies in different states that have found similar results. (See for instance Shyne and Schroeder [1978]; Magura [1979]; and Tatara, Shapiro, and Pettiford [1987].)

A number of other studies reveal the emotional and physical effects of foster care. For instance, children in foster care are three to six times more likely than children not in care to have emotional, behavioral, and developmental problems, including depression, impaired social relationships, and difficulties in school [Child Welfare League 1995]. Additionally, some estimates show that about 30% of the children in care have severe emotional problems. (See Tatara [1993] and Festinger [1994].)

According to a 1995 study by the U.S. General Accounting Office, 58% of young children in foster care had serious health problems, and 62% had been exposed to drugs from the mother while she was pregnant. With regard to educational needs, a variety of studies have indicated that children and young people in foster care tend to perform more poorly than children who are not in foster care, have lower educational attainment than the general population, and lag behind in their education by at least one year [Festinger 1994; GAO 1994].

It seems, then, that once placed into the foster care system, many children end up spending a large part of their childhood there. In the mid-1980s, some studies showed the length of time in care had shortened. By 1984, for example, based on data from 27 states, only 10% of the children in foster care had been there for six years or more [Tatara et al. 1987]. More recently, a study in New York finds that foster children have been in care for an average of 3.3 years [Coalition Voice 1994]. Part of the problem in accurately assessing this issue is the fact that computerized data to monitor the length of stay in foster care are not available and that nationwide data do not exist. Thus, researchers must examine the problem on a state-by-state basis. This is but one problem in the system, however.

One of the biggest problems is the frequent movement of children from one foster parent family to another. Tiffin [1982] has found that at least 50% of all foster children experience more than one move and at least 20% move three or more times. Fanshel and Shinn's [1986] study in New York City showed that, over a five-year period, 30% had experienced two foster care families and 28% lived with three or more different families. This study also showed a direct relationship between the length of time a child stays in foster care and the number of moves he or she undergoes while in the system. In other words, the longer children stay in foster care, the more times they can expect to move from family to family.

Thus, it seems that one interpretation of the research is that the length of time that children spend in foster care decreased. However, the research also tells us that many children experience three or more placements. The explanation for this is that, while children are staying in the foster care system for less continuous time, they are exiting and reentering the system at a faster rate.

The conclusion that can be drawn from this is that the foster care system in this country has become a type of revolving door, with children entering and exiting the system each year, in many cases, the same ones. The obvious psychological and emotional consequences this has on children should not be minimized. Issues such as low self-esteem, feelings of rejection, alienation from both the child's natural and foster parents, as well as issues of neglect and abuse, are common ones for foster children.

It seems that the immediate impact of foster care has negative implications: problems of separation and trauma seem to be clearly identified in the research. There is a great deal of variability in terms of the quality of foster care families and in the workers within the system, however. Moreover, this variation also extends to group homes and institutions as well. While some have deplorable conditions that should lead to their closing, others seems to maintain acceptable minimum standards.

Thus, it seems that, as Pelton [1988] states, the foster care system in this country is beset by a paradox. Because the emphasis has continued to be on reuniting the child with his or her parents whenever possible, even if the foster family provides a more stable and healthy environment, a self-fulfilling prophecy can easily emerge. Because it is viewed as a temporary arrangement, foster parents may be told not to get too attached to the child, because this will lead to eventual disappointment and problems of emotional separation.

In some cases this is relatively easy to do; especially if the child presents problems for the family. As a result, the child is soon on his or her way to another foster family, usually because the family contends the child is too difficult to handle. This usually results in move after move for the child, essentially for the same reasons. The child is never given the love or attention he or she needs and continues to act out, thereby causing additional problems. And the more moves the child makes, the more difficult he or she can become, thereby contributing to the cycle of despair inherent to the system.

On the other hand, at times the natural parents may be in an uncomfortable position. In some cases, they are prevented or discouraged from visiting the child in foster care, even though the goal may be to return the child to them at some point in the future. Consequently, some parents may decide not to visit them to allow them to adjust emotionally to the new situation. In short, the worker and/or the parent may determine that a lack of visits may be in the best interests of the child.

The upshot is that the child may interpret this lack of visitation as a sign that the parent no longer cares for her or him. The emotional upheaval this can cause may also lead to unruly and disruptive behavior, thus facilitating continuous movement from one foster home to another. Moreover, even if a parent does decide to remain close during the child's stay in foster care, if it is perceived as an obligatory visit, the end result is the same.

Foster Care in Connecticut

Until 1995, the basic philosophy of foster care in the State of Connecticut had been that, if at all possible, the child should be returned to the biological parent. The feeling was that the parent was in the best position to meet the long-term needs of the child. Recently, this has changed. In 1995, a new commissioner was appointed to the Department of Child and Families (DCF), whose primary concern is the safety of the child. This is true even if this means permanent separation from the biological parents. Additionally, the procedures by which children are placed in foster care have been modified as well.

According to sources in the DCF, in the 1970s, the policy concerning voluntary placement (which is when a parent agrees he or she can no longer care for his or her child, and asks the state to intervene), were outlined to some extent, such as the time limits on treatment plans, but there was an overall lack of adequate supervision of case workers, of children, and of the administrative tasks that accompany this type of placement. For instance, the 1967 policy relating to the supervision of children in Foster care, states that:

> Purposeful contacts to the child and the family (foster and natural) and/or responsible institutional staff, should be made as often as necessary, but at intervals not to exceed three months. To understand the child's feelings and thinking about himself and his situation, a personal interview with the child is necessary. Even young children give expression to their feelings through responses and behavior. The child should be seen and heard when available and where appropriate.... The plan for each child is reviewed and re-evaluated at least every six months, and the current evaluation and plan is recorded and dated in the case record. If the situation changes at any time which affects the plan this should be indicated and the review will relate to the changed plan, with the due date for the next review changed accordingly. Pertinent material may be duplicated and placed in the appropriate record, i.e., foster home or natural parent, etc.

Thus, while workers were required to submit the appropriate forms, there was a great deal of latitude on when and how often they visited homes, and even how and in what way they interviewed the children. Perhaps more important, while there was in fact a policy in place, many workers routinely ignored it. As a result, there was no way to determine how many children were in placement, how long they had stayed at any one home, or how many homes into which a child had been placed. The policy on commitment was also indefinite: the child would be in placement until he or she reached majority age. And when a child had been voluntarily placed, the parents did not usually receive a copy of the treatment plan, commitment papers, or any other documentation concerning their child's care.

One of the most important pieces of legislation concerning foster care policies was the Adoption Assistance and Child Welfare Act of 1980. This act was designed to alleviate what was referred to as foster care "drift," where the child would drift from one foster home to another. This act was amended in 1995, which increased the restrictions on foster care placement.

As of 1995, the policy concerning voluntary commitment is much more restrictive. When parents request commitment of their child to foster care, there is an initial plan that outlines the responsibilities of the parent (e.g., drug treatment or other therapies), and the state also documents their role in terms of child care as well as the various services offered to the parent. This plan is reviewed within 60 days with the parent, a service provider, and the worker. Together they assess what has been accomplished and what steps remain for the parent. If the parent fails to meet the parameters of the initial agreement, a petition is filed in court under the neglect and/or uncared for statutes. The child is then committed to the Commissioner of DCF for up to 18 months (a recent amendment to the act now stipulates that the time period is shortened to 12 months).

Within that time period, the worker has weekly contact with the parents to advise them on their progress and to help prepare them for the eventual return of the child. If no progress is made after the 18 months, the state files for a Termination of Parental Rights (TPR) and makes the child eligible for either adoption, permanent foster care, or guardianship by a relative.

While attempts are being made to modify the system to better protect the interests of the child, the scope of the problem has become greater. It may appear that the current policies and procedures are designed to eliminate the problems that many foster children have dealt with in the past; however, the nature of the problems have become more severe. While alcohol abuse among parents was a common problem in the 1970s that often resulted in abuse and/or neglect of the child, the problems have been exacerbated by the introduction of crack cocaine.

Thus, the nature of the dependency is much greater, which leads to frequent relapses. This, in turn, results in the aforementioned revolving door of foster care. While the changes will help to some degree, the problems encountered by many families are not easy ones to resolve. It seems obvious that the children are the ones who suffer from the nature of these problems, as well as from the faults that can be placed on the foster care system. In many ways, states continue to repeat the same mistakes over and over again. Children continue to be placed in homes that have been certified based on expediency rather than on adequate care, and many children are lost within a system that has never attempted to document the extent of the problem.

In an effort to identify the magnitude of this problem, in 1995 the DCF conducted a study of the 3,472 children in foster care. The goal was to interview 100% of the case record reports to identify the average length of time a child stays in a particular foster home, and how many times the child has been placed in foster care, as well as some of the particular problems they experience.

This study is one of the first of its kind and is designed to establish a benchmark for the future of foster care in Connecticut. As of this writing, the analysis is ongoing and the study is not yet completed. This effort is an honest attempt to understand the state's role in the process as well as to identify ways to improve current practices. On the other hand, while this study provides a glimpse of the nature of the problem, there is a large body of research that reminds us that self-evaluation is always problematic (see Rosenbaum and Lurigio [1987]).

Many employees are reluctant to engage in an honest assessment because of the possible backlash from their administrators. As such, what is needed is an objective and thorough examination of what is occurring in our foster care system, where the children end up, and ultimately what mechanisms are in place to require case workers and their supervisors to be made accountable for the care of those children.

Welcome to the Hotel California

With this information, it becomes relatively easy to see that my involvement in foster care was rather typical. The first stop on the state foster care express was in West Haven, Connecticut. As we drove up to the house, I was told that this family had received awards for the quality of their foster care. As we approached the house, something felt terribly wrong. The house was in shambles, both inside and out. There were cars parked in the backyard, some of which had been cannibalized to save others, the paint was peeling off the clapboards of the house and there was garbage strewn all over the front porch and the backyard. I thought we had the wrong address and said as much to my worker, Kathy. She smiled and told me that I should not judge a book by its cover. I grew even more concerned at that point.

Upon entering the house I was overwhelmed by the smell of cigarette smoke and animal odor. The family consisted of a husband and wife, both in their early fifties, a 15-year-old son, a 14-year-old daughter, and another daughter, a 7-year-old permanent foster child. In addition, there were several dogs and a few cats lying on the furniture or the floor. As I stood in the doorway wondering how I was going to survive in this environment, a squirrel monkey bounded down the stairway to my left and launched itself at my head. I ducked and the monkey landed right on Kathy's chest. I thought that should have solved the problem and we would be on our way in no time. I was wrong. I neglected to consider the fact that a moment's embarrassment by the worker could not and would not overcome a desperate need to clear me from her caseload. If she did not place me here, she would be stuck with me. I ended up staying almost a year, despite my continued protests over the treatment I received.

During my time there, I made every attempt to fit in. It was an Italian family, so I tried to form my relationships with them based on our common ethnicity. Unfortunately, this family was interested in me for two main purposes: the money my mother continued to pay each month and the amount of work I could perform around the house. The husband, who had until recently been the sole breadwinner in the family, had become disabled with severe leg injuries that had required extensive surgery. This not only meant that he could not work, but that his chores and projects around the house were not being completed either.

I also realized shortly after my arrival that there were a lot of the purchases around the house, such as clothes for the other kids, parts for the cars, tools, paint for the house, etc., all of which were new. It does not take a skilled observer of human behavior to figure out what was happening here. I was being taken to Railroad Salvage, a discount store in town, to buy cheap, irregular clothes and the biological kids were being sent to the Post Mall to buy new things. This differential treatment also applied to food, where two meals would be prepared: one for the family, which included cuts of meat, and one for me—hamburger. I complained to my mother about this type of treatment, as well as to Kathy. My mother's response was to tell Kathy that I was having trouble adjusting to the new family environment, which I did, and my worker did absolutely nothing. It was only when I threatened to call her supervisor that she visited the home. Of course, the family steadfastly denied any wrongdoing, even though I was still wearing old clothing and the kids were fashionably dressed. Still, the worker would not substantiate my claims.

In addition to this double standard, the husband and son started putting me to work around the house. Some of the tasks included sorting nails, grating the dirt lot they called a backyard, scraping and painting the outside of the house, digging holes and burying garbage, and cleaning the entire house while they went to the beach.

I honestly tried to make the best of this situation, but it was painfully obvious that they were ripping off everyone involved. A few months later I learned that this family was on welfare and were being given food stamps.

It was at that time that their motives became clear. It also became obvious that my worker had little or no interest in discovering how inept this family actually was in providing adequate care. The irony of this situation has never been lost on me: the fact that a family on welfare (and had been for some time as I later found out) was winning awards for being good foster parents when all they were doing was taking the money the state (in my case my mother) was giving them and improving their standard of living.

While I had my suspicions, I could not be sure if they were accurate. I decided to see if I was right. I started to refuse to clean the house while they went to the beach. I refused to work around the yard and stated I was willing to do only my share of the work, but no more. I began to take food off the dinner table that was not earmarked for my plate. And the situation exploded.

The husband began to take his frustration out on me. He walked around with a cane and started to swing it at my back or legs when I was looking in another direction. Occasionally, when he was really angry, he would swing it like a baseball bat. When he used this technique however, he would typically lose his balance and fall, which only enraged him (and everyone else) further. Since he was disabled I could not bring myself to retaliate against him, although there were many times when I was indeed tempted. Instead, I learned to keep my eyes on him at all times.

Sam, the 15-year-old son, waited until I came home from school and ambushed me, beating me until I promised I would obey his parents without question. This became a fairly frequent occurrence. I was a stubborn kid and was used to getting into fights; my time spent with my brothers on Frank Street had prepared me well. When the son began to include some of his friends in the attacks against me, however, it was a bit too much. Even though I had promised myself that I would try to make this work and avoid getting into trouble, I discovered that the situation was beyond my control. I began carrying a weapon again, a knife. I was not sure what would happen, but I knew I could not allow the beatings to continue. Sam and I slept in bunk beds, with my bed on top. Each night I wondered how long it would be before he started to hassle me.

During the day, I would get in trouble at school so that I would be required to spend time in detention hall. This kept me out of the house. Additionally, I searched around for any outside activity that would keep me away from them. I even joined the West Haven Chess Club, which held its meetings in the library down the street. I did not especially care for the games, but I knew that Sam or someone would be checking up on me. I learned a little about playing chess, but mostly I hung around the book stacks and read. I thought that the problems would subside as long as I stayed away from home for a good deal of time. I did not know what I was going to do during the summer, but that was quite a few months away and I had to deal with the present.

Unfortunately, the problems continued. The Ruttmans forbade me from going to the chess club meetings because I "had work to do" around the house. When I had to stay after school because of detention, they compounded my punishment by adding tasks to my work list. Any time I wanted to leave the home, I was punished. I had no friends outside the classroom (and only a few inside it). This had become a common occurrence for me, so it was not a great sacrifice. If I wanted to make friends and spend time with them, however, the family would not let me. This began to sound familiar: the Lawrence family had done the same thing. Thus, I began to think the avoidance strategy, based on the philosophy of cooperation, was not working. The problems remained the same. I knew that I could not remain passive and survive. So I did what my New Haven experience taught me to do: I attacked.

I informed my mother and Kathy about what was happening. When they called the family, both were assured that I was overreacting to some of the disciplinary measures they were employing. Given that I was a street kid, they said, I needed a little more aggressive therapy. This mollified my mother and Kathy, despite the fact that when my mother visited me, I would have black eyes, split lips, and other assorted bruises. The family would explain this away by saying I had gotten into a fight at school. All of this was believable, given the circumstances, but was absolutely not true. Since I was being given a label, I decided that I would live up to it. The punishment would still be severe, but at least I would feel as though I deserved it. More importantly, I would have had a chance to get a few licks in myself. And the war began.

The first night I decided to fix Sam once and for all. As he slept in his bunk I crept downstairs and outside to the woodpile. This was literally a stack of wood, 2x4s, 2x6s, 4x8s, and other lengths that were kept for various projects around the house. There were assorted scraps of wood that were left over when the original lengths were measured and cut. I grabbed a three-foot piece of 2x4 and quietly went back upstairs to my bedroom.

After hitting Sam in the ankles with the 2x4 a few times and then giving him my best Dave Kingman swing into the ribs as he sat up in pain, I whispered to him that if he ever hit me again or had any of his friends do it, he would find his monkey dead on the floor the next day. Sam's cries of pain awoke everyone in the house. Things settled down and Sam convinced everyone he had had a nightmare. The next day I smiled as he limped past me at breakfast and winced in pain when he sneezed.

The next few days went without incident until two police officers from the Welfare Fraud Division of the State Police showed up. It seems they were given an anonymous tip about someone falsely claiming dependents that did not exist. While this was not true, they did find other improprieties. Moreover, the income derived from my mother for my care, as well as several other dubious business deals, were never declared on the Ruttmans' income tax.

It was during this time that I had gotten in touch with my brother Mark, who had since married. His wife and my brother Daryl came to see me one day not long after I had spent the weekend with them. I had apprised them of the situation and hoped that someone would recognize what was happening and get me out of this environment. I realized that they were trying to put their lives back together, so I tried to make the situation sound somewhat manageable. I did not tell them anything about the violent nature of my time there, but did tell them that I was tired of being exploited.

Shortly thereafter, I went to live with Mark and his wife. This was a strange situation, since they were recently married and had no idea about how to raise a kid like me. I was far from the average 14-year-old and the likelihood of success was small. It did not last. There were an assortment of problems, all of which led Mark to contact my mother and ask that she take me back after about three months. She refused to do so even on a temporary basis. I think by this time she had begun to feel as though her time as a parent was over and that as long as she paid for my care, she was under no obligation to take me back. Since the state was obligated to find a licensed foster home for me, they decided to put me in a temporary foster home until more permanent arrangements were made.

The next stop was in a small town in the Nagatuck Valley section of the state. This family was a second marriage for the husband, the first for the wife and they had a son together, age 7. There were other children from the husband's first marriage, a 17-year-old who raced motorcycles, a 20-year-old daughter who did not live at home, and another son, approximately my age, who lived with his paternal grandmother. While I spent less than two months there, from late June to August, this was one of the happiest times I can remember.

I think the husband had some idea of the nature of my problems and that I harbored an awful lot of resentment towards people. I think he also sensed that what I needed was a chance to know someone without looking to protect myself or finding what they wanted from me. He was a kind man who taught me how to ride a motorcycle, a riding lawnmower, and I just began to develop a stable relationship with him when my worker found a permanent home. It was getting close to the beginning of school and my living situation needed to be settled.

She had tried to have me placed in a group home for emotionally disturbed kids (another label) but after meeting with the director of the home, as well as the in-house psychologist, both agreed that I did not belong in such an environment. I remember the psychologist telling me that there was no way I belonged in the home. By this time I had nothing but contempt for my worker anyway, so I reveled in the fact that she could not pawn me off on someone else. One of the things I recall saying to her was something akin to "What's the matter? Are you afraid you are going to have to do your job now?"

She fired back with a stare and a comment stating that if they could not find a place for me to stay, I might have to spend some time at an "institution" for boys. While it may have been designed to intimidate me, it had the opposite effect. I was anxious to get as far away from her and everyone else as possible. I had become self-reliant and knew that the problems I experienced with other families had honestly not been my fault. The situation in West Haven proved that to me. I realized that these people, as well as my mother and my worker, were only interested in making their lives as easy as possible. If that meant that I was exploited, abused, or neglected, so be it. If that meant that I would be placed in a home for kids with serious psychiatric problems and I could be damaged further as a result, so what? It was not their problem. They had their own agendas and their own lives to enjoy. What was one more teenager anyway? Besides, it was not as though I endeared myself to people, not as though I made it easy for them to place me. I was an angry young man in their eyes. I was angry all right. Angry at the injustices that had been inflicted upon me by my own family, made to feel as though I should be grateful to people who took advantage of me, and made to feel as though all the problems I experienced were of my doing—so much so that when I asked for help no one would come to my aid. Yes, I was an angry young man, but not in the way that most people thought. I kept reminding myself over and over again that if I ever got the chance to get out of this situation, I would jump at the opportunity. People were trying to make me be someone I was not and could not be.

Thank God I'm Not a Country Boy

In August 1974, I learned that my next home was a farm in Connecticut. Kathy had found an elderly couple who owned a farm and were willing to take me in. I balked at this situation from the beginning. I knew nothing about living on a farm and had no inclination to learn. I was from the city and liked that environment better than any other. Kathy read me the "riot act" and told me there was absolutely no other place for me to go. Besides, she said, I might learn to like country living. To prove her point, she arranged to have me stay with this couple for a weekend. Had I thought about it for a moment, I would have realized that this was simply a prelude to what amounted to a certainty: I had no choice in the matter. She was simply attempting to pacify me by saying if I did not like it, I could always leave.

This family consisted of a husband and wife, the former was 70 years old and the latter 65, a 25-year-old son who attended college at the state university, and another son, who was in his late twenties, married, with two children, and lived near his parents.

I had suspicions about this arrangement, especially since the younger son spent most of his time away at school. Given the husband's age, I thought it was odd that they would willingly take in a 14-year-old "city slicker," as they used to call me. I suspected it had more to do with free labor than anything else. As it turned out, I was right. By this point in the game, I was familiar with this tactic. Take the boy in, make him feel welcome for a while. Then begin to ask him to do a few chores around the house, phrasing it in way that would be akin to "it would be a big help to everyone." Then gradually the list would grow longer and longer and the expectation changed from it being a favor to an obligation. And if the boy questions this or refuses to complete his jobs, remind him how grateful he should be because this family did not have to take him in, but did so out of the goodness of their hearts. And if that still does not work, threaten to withhold privileges or smack him around a little.

Thus, when the game began I was several steps ahead of everyone else. During the two and a half years I lived on this farm, it became clear that I was to be considered hired help. What made it easy to disguise this fact was the environment. A farm is a place where lots of work needs to be done to maintain it. As such, a young boy could be expected to perform any number of tasks on a daily, weekly, or monthly basis. Unlike the Ruttmans' home in West Haven, where it was difficult to justify (although obviously not to my worker or my mother) the nature and the amount of work I was required to do, on the farm it was different. The argument could be made that hard work was just what a young man like me needed to "straighten out." Thus, as my chores increased, it was justified based on a strategy of discipline and an attempt to instill in me a work ethic. This was complete nonsense.

While they may have convinced my clueless social worker and my mother, I saw what was happening. They were not interested in my well-being or in restoring my self-confidence or anything of the sort. This became clear to me when I decided I did not want to work on the farm, but wanted to get involved in typical junior high school activities.

As I began to learn more about the new school, I decided that I wanted to play football. Some of my friends were playing and they encouraged me to join. I kept hearing from my worker, my mother, and from the Cross family, how I needed to become "better adjusted" to my environment. I had always liked playing football and although I had never played anything other than sandlot games, I thought it might be fun.

When I conveyed my feelings to the Crosses, however, it was met with silent, hostile stares. I was told that it would be my responsibility to get to and from the practices and games, and that my chores would still need to be finished when I returned home. Moreover, after the games, my teammates usually met at a restaurant for pizza to celebrate or commiserate. I was forbidden from going to any of these outings. What is interesting about this turn of events was that both of the sons had played football in junior and high school and both stated they looked upon their experience as a pleasant one. The husband and wife went to the games and cheered for them: it was a family affair. This was clearly a departure from the standard used with their own children, who were given rides to and from games and practices and were exempted from chores during the week.

The Crosses did everything they could to discourage me from playing on the team. Since I was required to remain after school for practice, I could not take the bus home, some eight miles away. As such, I asked if they would pick me up from practice. They refused. My mother had bought me a ten-speed bicycle for my birthday that year and I was told by the

Crosses that if I wanted to play football, I was going to have to get myself to and from practices on my own. Each morning I would ride the eight miles, mostly downhill, to school, lock my bike, and go to class. After school I would endure the grueling practices and then ride my bike up the mountain to the farm. This was true even as the days grew shorter and it became dark around 5 P.M. There were many evenings when I was so tired from the day's events that I had to stop and sit on the side of the road and rest.

On game days, while my teammates had their parents and siblings cheering them on, I stood on the sidelines and never bothered to look into the stands. The Crosses had already made it clear that they would not attend any of the games. Several times I relied on the generosity of my neighbors, some of whom had sons or daughters in the band or the cheerleading squad, to give me a ride home. I think they sensed what was happening but were unable or unwilling to say anything. They helped when they could, by taking me to hockey games, letting me get away from the farm for a short time, and when they saw me, threw my bicycle in the back of their station wagons and gave me a ride home. They were good people who cared and I will never forget their generosity.

Another tactic the Crosses used to discourage me from extracurricular activities was to punish me for missing dinner during football season, which began in late August and ended by Thanksgiving. Each night I would not return home until well after 7 P.M., largely because it took me so long to ride home. While practice usually ended around 5:30 or 6:00 P.M., by the time I showered, dressed, and got out of the locker room, it was usually 6:00 or 6:30 P.M.. Then I had to make my trek with the bicycle, which often took an hour or more. Because I missed dinner (and for some reason Mrs. Cross continued to leave my plateful of food on the table even though she knew I would not be home for hours), I was given an extra chore to do around the house that weekend. Since this happened every night, I could expect five additional things to do on the weekends. Each time I was admonished with the phrase, "Well, you want to play football, this is what it gets you." Add to the fact that I was frequently injured and did not play much, and it was difficult to remain on the team.

But by this point in our relationship I realized what their motivations were and did not become discouraged about their stoic hostility towards my decision to play. By then I knew they had brought me to the farm to compensate for Mr. Cross's declining health. And in reality, it was a great setup for them: they were given a young kid who could work the farm for them and they not only were thanked by the state for giving them the opportunity, they received $130 a month.

Once again, I began to rebel at this treatment. Kathy continued to tell me that there were no other places for me to go. When I asked her what the state would do if this family began abusing me, she had no answer. Obviously, if this occurred, they would have found some other place for me to live. Again, a classic case of expediency. She simply could not be bothered. My mother visited on Sundays, now with her boyfriend, her ex-boss at the diner in Chichester. That explained an awful lot about that situation. When I told her what was happening to me, she tried to placate me a bit and then go on to another subject. I think she did not want this responsibility to begin with and as her relationship with her boyfriend developed, she became less and less interested in meeting her responsibilities. She always talked about moving to Florida and retiring, but I never gave it much thought. Little did I know that it was part of the bigger plan.

Her boyfriend was married but in the process of getting a divorce. He had three children (all of them lived with their mother), with whom he was close. I often wondered if his need to spend time with them resulted in my mother's decision to include me as well. It would be difficult to justify spending all her free time with his kids. How could she explain away the fact that I was living with someone she did not even know and could not find the time to spend with me? Thus, if anything, I think her visits were motivated more by guilt than a great desire to see me. Unfortunately, the situation deteriorated even further. I would complain about the way I was treated only to be told there was nothing anyone could do. I thought otherwise: I felt that if no one else was willing to look out for me, I would do it myself. I started to run away.

During those heated moments when the Crosses and I argued, I casually commented about the implications if I were injured in an automobile accident while riding my bike home from school. I also commented that if it were discovered that this was due to their negligence, they would be held responsible. This would usually send them into a rage and the yelling and screaming escalated. My response was usually a question about whether their screaming indicated they were nervous. This sent them over the edge and they ordered me to my room. It was a place I had become familiar with, and I appreciated the sanctuary, even though it was an extension off their bedroom. I had to walk through their room to get to mine, which made it somewhat inconvenient, but there was a door and I did have some degree of privacy. When I realized the situation would not improve, I decided that I was the only person responsible for my care and that any abuse that took place was my own fault for allowing it to happen.

Running Away Again

On several occasions, before leaving in the morning, I grabbed some additional food, a flashlight, some clothes, and a sleeping bag, put them in my backpack, and headed to school. I had come to like the school environment, where I could be left alone in the library and study. I had a few friends by this time and knew quite a few others. My teammates were friendly towards me and I was grateful for that affiliation. I also had a great deal of respect for my coach, Dan Hartmann, who seemed to treat people with dignity and never let them get down on themselves too much. Still, I did not want to go home.

There was a wooded area with a stream of sorts that ran behind the school. It was a place where a lot of kids went when they were skipping classes or playing hookey. It seemed safe and quiet. I would unroll my sleeping bag, make a fire at night, and enjoyed the peace and quiet. I also enjoyed knowing that the Crosses were probably going crazy looking for me. Not that they were concerned for my welfare, but because they were afraid of what might happen to them if the state learned what was going on. I can still recall the sounds of the stream and the crackle of the fire while I sat there and ate my bologna sandwiches. I read my books and did my homework by flashlight, and in the morning snuck into the gym before anyone arrived. I showered and got ready for school and then carried on the next day as if nothing had happened. When I eventually returned home, I would get into all kinds of trouble with the Crosses, but I knew it was hollow: it was not out of concern for me.

After a while, my campsite seemed to be too risky. I had spent several nights there and thought it might be time to find a new place. I found a great spot down the street from school. It was near one of the pizza places that I was forbidden to go to after our football games. It was a wooded area that belonged to the power company. There were pine trees and another stream and many "No Trespassing" signs. I figured the power company did not patrol the area, thinking the signs would be an adequate deterrent. I spent many nights there as well. I knew that the situation at the farm could not last, however. When I did go home they threatened to take my bike away from me, to call the police and have me arrested, and, of course, increased my chores that weekend. I knew they would not call the police or the state because I would tell them what had been going on. Then they would lose their hired hand and the money they earned every month. No, they would keep quiet. I also knew they would never tell anyone that I had been running away for the same reason.

Getting Dumped

Eventually, I knew that something had to be done: I had to convince my mother to get me out of this place. The next Sunday she visited I was ready to tell her everything and make an impassioned plea to get out. My timing of events was awful: it was that same Sunday that she told me she had awarded custody of me to the state and that she and her boyfriend were moving to Florida. She mollified me a bit by saying that once she was settled and found a job, she would send for me. But in the interim, the state would be ultimately responsible for my care. It did not change anything, she said. She was still my mother. The only difference was that now the state would pay the bills. I was not convinced that this was the complete truth, but what choice did I have? I would not be seeing her on Sundays any longer since she would be moving at the end of the month. I was stunned at this turn of events. I had never given any thought to this possibility. I had suspected that she was interested in other things, but not that she would completely shirk her responsibilities. And to be honest, I did hold a glimmer of hope that we would be reunited as a family again. Little did I realize that I was not part of the plan.

After she left, the situation with the Crosses became more intense. I think they must have felt that I was vulnerable because of my mother's departure and to be fair, that was true. I was taken so off guard that I could not focus. Deep down I knew that she was leaving and had no intention of sending for me. But I did not want to believe it. What this meant, however, was that I was completely dependent on the state and my social worker, a frightening thought. Now I had no advocate at all. In the past I had felt that I could call my mother if my worker was being completely unreasonable, but now even that was gone. I was really on my own.

It took me a while to get over this development. During that time, I had started talking to my coach about my situation. He seemed interested and concerned about my well-being. For some reason, and I do not know why, I trusted him. In light of what I had been through, I had no reason to trust anyone. I continued to run away and the treatment at the farm continued, but talking to him made it feel a little better. He never said much, and to this day, he still says little, but he continues to have a calming effect on me.

I had found a brochure for the U.S. Navy in the library one day and thought a lot about joining. I thought this was a good way to get out of this whole mess and at the same time, have a career. I thought I wanted to be an MP in the Army, but the Navy had some sort of appeal to me. I did not know what I wanted to do, but I watched a John Wayne-type movie on the Navy Seabees (the Navy's version of the construction crew), and thought it might be fun. Parenthetically, I had shown a little talent in my shop classes in school and thought this might be a possible career.

The only problem was that I was under age: the only way they would accept a minor would be with parental consent. This would be tricky since I had not seen my father in years and my mother was frolicking around the beaches of Florida. I had given some thought to forging her signature and signing up. I went to my coach one day and talked to him about it. We talked for a while and then he told me that he wanted me to come and see him the next day. I am not sure if I ever told him this, but I was on the verge of making a permanent break from the farm that night. I was going to run away and then somehow try to get into the Navy the next morning. If that did not work, I planned to return to Frank Street and see if I could convince my grandfather to take me in. If that failed, at least I would be in an environment that I was comfortable: I remember thinking I could always sleep with Queenie again.

At any rate, out of respect for my coach I went to see him the next day. He dropped a bomb on me that changed my entire life. He said he talked it over with his wife and they agreed that I could live with them for as long as I wanted. He said he would make all the necessary arrangements with the state and take care of all the details. I was absolutely shocked. I could not speak, I did not know what to say, and for some reason, for the first time in my life, I did not try to determine his motives. I had become used to looking for an angle when I dealt with people, simply because there was usually some sort of ulterior motive in their behavior toward me. Here I was so shocked that I did not even ask what was in it for him. I remember the next few moments as a blur, and the next thing I recall was bounding across the gym feeling as though my problems were over. I finally had the chance I was looking for to live a normal life. As I was to discover, however, not everyone shared my enthusiasm.

References

Child Welfare League of America. (1995). *Foster care F.Y.I.* Washington, DC: Author.

Coalition Voice. (1994). *Foster care facts.* New York: Citizens' Coalition for Children, Inc.

Fanshel, D., & Shinn, E. B. (1978). *Children in foster care.* New York: Columbia University Press.

Festinger, T. (1994). *The foster children of California.* Sacramento, CA: The Children's Services Foundation.

Gruber, A. R. (1978). *Children in foster care: Destitute, neglected and betrayed.* New York: Human Sciences Press.

Magura, S. (1979). Trend analysis in foster care. *Social Work Research and Abstracts, 15,* 29-36.

Mass, H. S. (1969). Children in long-term foster care. *Child Welfare, 48,* 321-33.

Pelton, L. H. (1988). *For reasons of poverty.* Westport, CT: Praeger.

Pelton, L. H. (1978). *Children in need of decisions: Foster children and the alternatives of continued foster care, return home, and adoption.* Trenton, NJ: Bureau of Research, New Jersey Division of Youth and Family Services.

Rosenbaum, D., & Lurigio, A. (1987). *Community crime prevention.* Thousand Oaks, CA: Sage.

Shyne, A. W., & Schroeder, A. G. (1978). *National study of social services to children and their families.* Washington, DC: U.S. Children's Bureau.

Tartara, T., Shapiro, P., & Pettiford, E. (1993). *Characteristics of children in substitute and adoptive care.* Washington, DC: U.S. Government Printing Office.

Tartara, T., Shapiro, P., & Pettiford, E. (1987). *Characteristics of children in substitute and adoptive care.* Washington, DC: American Public Welfare Association.

Tiffin, S. (1982). *In whose best interest? Child welfare reform in the progressive era.* Westport, CT: Greenwood Press.

U.S. General Accounting Office. (1994). *Foster care: Health care need of many young children are unknown and unmet.* Washington, DC: U.S. Government Printing Office.

U.S. General Accounting Office. (1976). State intervention on behalf of neglected children. *Stanford Law Review, 28,* 623-706.

Further Readings on Foster Care

Connecticut State Welfare Department. (1967). *Internal document: Services for children manual,* Vol. 2, Chapter 4, 325-327. New Haven, CT: Author.

Ferguson, T. (1966). *Children in care and after.* London: Oxford University.

Ferguson, T. (1983). *No one ever asked us: A postscript to foster care.* New York: Child Welfare League of America.

Kadushin, A. (1972). *Child welfare services.* New York: Macmillan.

Knitzer, J., Allen, M. L., & McGowan, B. (1978). *Children without homes.* Washington, DC: Children's Defense Fund.

Wald, M. S., Carlsmith, J. M., & Leiderman, P. H. (1988). *Protecting abused and neglected children.* Stanford, CA: Stanford University Press.

7

Culture Shock
and Labeling

When I learned that Dan wanted me to stay with him, I somehow felt that I had finally turned the corner: things were going to be better from this point on. When I returned home that afternoon, I immediately ran to the phone to call my social worker. Kathy had contacted me a few days earlier to tell me that the Crosses were no longer able to care for me. They cited the declining health of John, the husband, as well as the health problems of the wife's mother, who was staying with them at the time. My response was indifference. I told Kathy that the time had come to leave, since I was tired of being treated like a slave and that I had solved the problem. I knew Kathy wanted to get rid of me as fast as possible, so proposing an alternative seemed like something to which she would be receptive. Here I was telling her that I had a family that was willing to take a troubled teenage boy into their home... what could be better? I felt that I had done her job for her and was about to make her life much easier.

Kathy's response was that the family would have to be certified before any living arrangements could be made. This seemed like a trivial administrative detail to me and I dismissed it. I assumed that they would want to interview Dan, Maryann, and their two daughters, Leslie and Tracy, as well as visit the home to ensure the conditions were acceptable. I could not imagine that this would be a problem, given how easily the workers had overlooked substandard homes in the past. I thought that if they were willing to place me with an abusive welfare family, or to place me in a situation that was clearly one in which I was an indentured servant, getting the Hartmanns certified would be a breeze. Wrong again.

Temporary Shelter

In the meantime, I needed a place to stay. This was January 1976 and I was still in school. As a result, arrangements were made for me to stay with an elderly woman who had a history of taking care of foster children, some of whom had emotional problems. I suppose I fit into that category, especially since my outbursts tended to be vocal. Was I mentally ill? I honestly do not think so. Was I an angry young man with a lot of emotional baggage? Of course. Had I been taken advantage of by many people along the way, including my family? The answer seems obvious. Was I suspicious and not trusting? Who would not be in my situation? This was the only way that I was able to survive.

When I arrived at this home, Kathy made it clear to me that this was strictly a temporary arrangement. I was to finish out the school year at Sleeping Giant Junior High and then I would move in with the Hartmanns. When I arrived at the Douglass home, I quickly realized that I would be the oldest member of this temporary family. There were two girls, both sisters, who had serious emotional problems.

Darlene was 11 years old and a bit overweight. She was also extremely sensitive and burst into tears at the slightest provocation. She went out of her way at times to please people, even when she did not have to. I think her weight problems stemmed largely from a lack of self-esteem. She desperately wanted to be liked by everyone and when this did not happen, she compensated by eating.

Her sister, Berta, was rail-thin and a real troublemaker. She was a devious sort who liked to create situations that would get other people in trouble, especially her sister. She was intolerant of Darlene and chastised her constantly. Berta was also precocious, and thought a lot more about sex than a 10-year-old should. She had a terrible crush on me and followed me wherever I went. She would try to come into my room at night to sleep next to me. After one such incident, I started locking my bedroom door. In the morning I would find her sleeping outside my door, curled up in a blanket leaning against the wall. I would then pick her up, carry her into her bedroom, and lay her back in her own bed. It was a little strange for me because I had not encountered anyone who cared for me that much.

There was one other member of our family, James. He was a 12-year-old boy who thought he could scam his way through life. He was always trying to think of ways to make money and I once told him he would end up as a used car salesman. He never wanted to work hard and never put much effort into anything. He was a bright guy in many ways, but he just did not want to pay his dues like everyone else. He continually got into some scrape or another with people over money. Not a weekend went by without someone coming to the house looking for him because he owed them money. A successful con man he was not.

James also had the run of the house until I arrived. Darlene and Berta were permanent placements while the woman, who I always referred to as Mrs. Douglass, was trying to decide if she could control him enough to make him permanent as well. James had been run through the system like I had and even spent some time in a group home. This was one of the last stops for him and I think Mrs. Douglass knew that, which was why she kept delaying her decision about him, hoping he would straighten out.

The woman was not at all wealthy: in fact she survived on a meager income. Her husband had passed away many years before and her only child, a daughter, lived next door with her husband and children. This home was where I was first introduced to powdered milk and all the bread I could eat. Mrs. Douglass would go shopping with her daughter once a week and would stop off at the bakery thrift shop and buy tens of loaves of bread. She would freeze them and this made up the bulk of our breakfast meals and snacks. If we were ever hungry, we could eat as much toast as we wanted.

He's Risky Business

Just before I left the farm, someone, probably my dimwitted case worker, thought it would be a good idea if I were given a battery of psychological tests to determine if I had some sort of mental disorder. After several years in their care, and after learning about my life up to that point, it finally occurred to someone that this might be a good idea.

According to state records, I met with a psychologist on January 16, 1976, five days before I was to be sent to the Douglass home. According to the documents, the psychological areas tested were intellectual, organic brain functions, and a personality diagnosis. I was given the Rorschach test as well as the Bender Gestalt and the Gordon Interview Inventory. At the time I was told it was an IQ test. The psychologist joked that he simply wanted to see how smart I was. As a result, I simply played around with him and his staff, and filled out the forms without giving any thought to what the answers were.

I had also become so callous to the state's way of doing things, I felt they had no right to know this information. Here I was, a 15-year-old kid, who was literally ignored by the state and my worker, who (despite repeated complaints of mistreatment) placed me in a home that was physically and emotionally abusive, and who did not seem at all interested in my best interests. And suddenly they want to know how smart I was. In my mind, I said to myself that they did not deserve any more information from me at all. So I screwed around with the tests.

What Do the Tests Tell Us?

One of the most familiar psychological tests to the average person, the Rorschach test utilizes ten cards, on each of which is printed a symmetrical inkblot. Five of the blots are in shades of gray and black only; two contain additional touches of bright red and the remaining three combine several pastel shades. As the respondent is shown each one, he or she is asked to tell what the blot could represent. Following the presentation of all ten cards, the examiner questions the individual systematically regarding the parts and aspects of each blot to which the associations were given. Here the respondents have an opportunity to clarify and elaborate their earlier responses.

In theory at least, the clinician is supposed to focus on the final global description of the individual, but in practice the information is derived from outside sources, such as other tests, interviews, and case histories. At best then, this test gives a rough sketch of the person's thought patterns, ideas, etc.

The Bender Visual Motor Gestalt Test, more commonly known as the Bender Gestalt Test, is widely used by clinical psychologists, predominantly for diagnosing brain damage as well as many types of psychopathology, such as schizophrenia and depression. This test consists of nine simple designs shown on cards individually. The respondent is instructed to copy each design, with the sample before him. In the process of copying the figures, subjects make errors which, it is assumed, are not simply a function of a lack of artistic skill and these distortions form the basis of the clinical interpretation of the Bender-Gestalt [Murphy & Davidshofer 1991]. Although for many years the test was administered by Bender and others to children who showed a variety of intellectual and emotional disorders, the data were not reported in objective and systematic form and were difficult to evaluate. In other words, the scoring of the test is more subjective than objective.

The Gordon Personality Inventory, which may have been called the Gordon Interview Inventory at the time I took the test, is essentially a forced choice exam that requires the respondent to choose between two descriptive terms or phases that appear equally acceptable but differ in validity. The paired phrases may be both desirable or both undesirable. The person must indicate which phrase is most and least characteristic of him- or herself. According to Anastasi [1988] this item form is rarely employed in personality inventories and there are several other tests that yield more accurate results.

The psychologist, for all his diagnostic tests, and all his glib comments during the interview, interpreted these test scores and diagnosed me as a "borderline schizo-paranoid" type and that I was a threat to myself and to anyone that lived with me. Again, these tests were subjective in their orientation and were not supplemented by other indicators. No objective indicators to measure intelligence were used, such as the Minnesota Multiphasic Personality Inventory (MMPI), the Edwards Personal Preference Schedule (EPPS), or even the Personality Research Form (PRF), all of which have been widely used for quite some time [Anastasi 1988].

The Upshot of the Tests

I had my suspicions about this guy, especially since he seemed too familiar with my background as well as with the Cross family. I began to wonder if they had told him more about me before I showed up. Then the tests, which I admittedly did not take seriously, "confirmed" what he had heard from others. I cannot say this is true for certain, but when the guy greets the Crosses by their first name and asks about the sons and the grandchildren, I thought something was up. So I was a psycho, at least as far as they were concerned. Moreover, my IQ was around 80 and I was classified as borderline mentally retarded. As a result of this diagnosis, the psychologist recommended immediate institutionalization and that I not be allowed anywhere near children.

This recommendation did not help me in my attempt to live with the Hartmanns. Suddenly the state was balking at letting me live with them. Of course, they were still trying to negotiate with the Crosses to allow me to remain with them. (Go figure that one out.) I was unstable and a paranoid schizo, who could not be allowed to be around children, but it was okay for me to live on a farm with two elderly people who would be unable to defend themselves if I were to suddenly lose touch with reality. Something smelled bad indeed. The Crosses continued to say they no longer wanted to keep me, but for some reason my worker kept trying to convince them to change their minds. When she relayed this information to me, and said that I was not going to be able to live with the Hartmanns, I was devastated. I felt that my entire world had come crashing down. To be given a glimmer of hope that things would be okay, to be told that I had a chance at a normal life, and then to have it snatched away, was overwhelming. I remember I spent the afternoon walking around the neighborhood and around Ridge Road in Hamden. I started to blame myself: I thought that perhaps there was something terribly wrong with me. Maybe the workers and the psychologist were right. Perhaps it would be best for me to spend time in an institution. I felt utterly drained, defeated, and completely discouraged. I had solved my own problem only to be kicked in the face by people who did not seem to care about me at all. And then I became quite angry.

I returned home and began packing my only suitcase. This piece of luggage originally belonged to my mother. She left it for me one day in the apartment at City Point and I had kept it ever since. It was small, with red and orange flowers. Actually, it was one of the ugliest suitcases ever produced in this country, but it was the only thing I had that I could really call my own. Given that it was not exactly overflowing with clothing, it was portable.

I decided then that I was going to get away from everyone: I was taking complete control over my life. My father had screwed it up when he had it, my mother botched things time after time when she was in charge, and the state set new standards for incompetence during their tenure. I had lived on the streets before, knew how to survive, and I would do it again. This time my plan was to run away and find a place to hang out for a while. Then I would simply forge my mother's signature and join the Navy like I had originally planned. At least I knew where I would be sleeping and getting my meals.

But before I did that, I felt I owed the Hartmanns a phone call apologizing for all that they went through and to thank them for trying to help me. This was one of the few times in my life that I cried out of emotion and not out of pain. To me, these were two different types of crying. I had seen a lot of really tough guys cry like babies when they were seriously hurt. But to cry out of despair was another thing altogether for me—it showed weakness. It was an indication of a lack of control, and it was unmanly. This was a lesson learned from my father, I guess.

I cried out loud for what seemed like an hour. I was hidden in a wooded cove and sobbed myself to sleep. When I awoke it was dark and I was freezing. I made my way back to Mrs. Douglass's home and tried to call the Hartmanns. They were not home and I vowed I would not run away until I had talked to them. Fortunately, it was the right thing to do.

A Reprieve

The next day I received a phone call from my case worker. We talked for a while and I tried to tell her that I did not want to lose my chance to live with the Hartmanns. I also said that I thought the tests were unfair since I did not take them seriously. She seemed genuinely surprised at this. I told her the story of how the psychologist and his staff informed me that the tests were to measure IQ and as such, I did not answer honestly and intentionally fabricated responses. She seemed a bit skeptical but professional ethics must have forced her to consider the possibility. When I mentioned the obvious relationship between the Crosses and the psychologist, and gave her details and examples to substantiate my claim, she agreed to contact another therapist.

Months after I had moved in with them, Dan and Maryann recounted what was happening to them during this time period. They too were asked to submit to an interview with the case worker to determine their viability as foster parents. The case workers were also required to visit their home to ensure that it was a safe environment in which to place me. I still think it is odd that so much effort was exerted to certify the Hartmanns, yet there were less qualified and even abusive foster parents that were not inspected. If their job is to detect problems or potential hazards, as well as identifying the obvious ones, why did they not recognize the Cross home for what it was? Why did they allow the Ruttman family in West Haven to remain eligible as foster parents when that situation was easy to identify as detrimental to children? The dilapidated conditions of the home and the disarray in backyard were clearly risks to minors. Moreover, while the fact that they were on welfare would not automatically exclude them from candidacy, it certainly raises the question about whether or not there was an economic incentive for them to take me in.

Add to the fact that I was dressed differently than the other children should have signaled to even the least informed that inequities existed. Yet my worker was willing to overlook these things. Now they were putting my only hope at a normal life in jeopardy by interviewing the Hartmanns and inspecting their home to make sure it "looked lived in." This was the criterion they used. It could not be too dirty or too clean, rather it had to appear to be lived in. Whatever that means. Not to mention it gives an incredible amount of authority to the particular inspector. The potential for abuse of discretion was, and is, widespread.

The interviews with Mr. Hartmann did not go well. According to his recollection, he visited the Department of Child and Youth Services office for his interview. The worker asked him to tell her about himself and he replied, "I was born, I grew up, and here I am." And that is all the information she received. One has to know Dan to appreciate the significance of this comment. Today we laugh at how this whole affair transpired, but at the time, it was no laughing matter. The worker tried several times to elicit additional information, but was unsuccessful.

In the meantime, I was still going to school at Sleeping Giant. Every Monday I would leave school early and walk about a block and a half to the psychologist's office. Initially, I was prepared for the same type of tests and the same curious stares that I had received the last time I was interviewed. On my first visit to the psychologist, the one who misdiagnosed me, I felt as though I were an alien and the scientists were staring at me in wonderment, as if trying to figure out which planet I came from. This time I thought I would have to endure the same indignities, but I was wrong again. Parenthetically, this was the most confusing time of my life. Everything I expected to happen did not, and things I could not begin to comprehend or understand were happening somewhat regularly.

Dr. Stephens was not at all what I expected. He would always greet me at the door and help me with my coat. Then we would walk back into his office and talk. The conversation never centered around my problems, my intelligence, or anything else that I thought he needed to know to make a diagnosis. Rather, we would simply talk about sports, the weather, my trouble with algebra (which was the class that I missed by seeing him every week). We spent a lot of time talking about woodshop. I had taken a course in woodworking and found I was fairly adept at these tasks. I made salad bowls on the wood lathe, jewelry boxes out of mahogany, and as a final project decided I wanted to tackle something difficult, a stepladder. I had read the plans and realized there were a lot of things to consider and the project would be time consuming. My teacher was encouraging and spent a lot of time with me. He even asked me to stay after class a number of times to help him with a few of his own projects. He was one of Mr. Hartmann's good friends and I wondered if he was just trying to help me in his own way.

At any rate, I worked hard on my ladder, and Dr. Stephens and I would talk about some of the problems I was having, how I planned to finish it, or to whom I would give it when completed. I spent another marking period in metalshop, where I learned to make cast-iron figures, sheet metal products, cold metal chisels, and worked on the metal lathe. I began to produce quite a number of things, most of which I gave away. I gave Dan a set of chisels, Brad received a cast-iron eagle mounted on walnut, and I gave my Mark the stepladder.

These types of conversations dominated our time together. Finally I asked him when he was going to start testing me to see if I was a psycho. By this time we were nearing the end of the school year and I began to wonder what was going to happen to me. Finally, on what turned out to be the last day I saw him, Dr. Stephens called me into his office and was extremely serious. I thought something had gone terribly wrong. He seemed upset and angry. Finally he composed himself and began to tell me what was going on. After the conversation I wanted to cry. I went home and wrote down what he said so I would never forget it. As the years went by, I would read these words again and again, especially when things were not going well. Dr. Stephens said that whoever had tested me before was, in his words, "an idiot." He continued, saying

> You are not a borderline schizo-paranoid type. You are a young man who has faced a lot of adversity and had weathered it remarkably well. In fact I'm surprised you have made it this far. Almost everyone you have come in contact with has mistreated you and betrayed your trust, even your own family. You are not a threat to Mr. Hartmann's children or anyone else. In all my years of therapy I have

never bucked the state before. I have always gone along with what they have said. But in this case, they are absolutely wrong and I'm going to buck them now.

I never saw Dr. Stephens again, nor did I ever have the opportunity to see the letter he wrote in my behalf. It must have worked, however, because shortly thereafter, Kathy called me and told me that the Hartmanns had been approved and that I was going to move in with them in July.

I was elated. I hugged Mrs. Douglass, the kids, anybody who was nearby. I finally had a chance to get out from under the rock. While I would still have to deal with Kathy, and I would have to return to Chichester (a place that held many bad memories for me and my family), I felt that all of those things would work themselves out. I was on my way.

Culture Shock

It was difficult in some ways to leave the Douglass home. I was only there a short time, but I had grown close to Darlene and Berta. They needed me and I was leaving. I wondered how many times that had happened in their lives. I was also a little sad to leave James. He was a pain in the butt and had some emotional baggage of his own, but basically he was an okay guy. He and I fought a lot, verbally and physically, but most of it was kid stuff. Nevertheless, I knew my time there had ended.

When I moved in with the Hartmanns I had no idea what to expect. Would they accept me? Would the two daughters, aged 5 and 6, be afraid of me? How was I supposed to act? I had lived in so many places before this and never really gave it much thought. After a while I knew the routine, but this was different. I was nervous. Perhaps I was putting more pressure on myself to make this work. I felt that this was my last shot—if I screwed it up or it did not work out, I did not know what would happen to me. I could accept the situation if it simply did not work out, but I did not want to contribute to it in any way.

Dan must have sensed my concern. When I arrived and had a chance to unpack, he gave me a tour of the house and ended it by saying, "There is the refrigerator. If you are hungry, you don't have to ask, just take it. The television is downstairs. If you want to watch it, go ahead. This is your home now. You don't have to worry about all that other stuff anymore." Those words, like the ones by Dr. Stephens, have always remained in the forefront of my memory.

I had played football for Sleeping Giant during my last year, ninth grade, and thought that I wanted to continue while at Chichester High School. This town was in an affluent part of Connecticut and the educational system in 1977 was considered by many people in town to be one of the better ones in the state. According to school documents, during my tenure from 1977-1979, about 345 students graduated each year. Of those, the percentage who went on to college averaged 76%. This is remarkable, given that the national average is only about 20%. During this same time period, the average SAT scores was 944 (454 verbal and 490 math). Additionally, the average IQ score for those years was 108. Now, I have never placed much emphasis or value in standardized tests. I feel they are a better indicator of testing ability and class bias than intelligence. However, some people use them as a marker of how well a person will do in an academic setting. While there were indeed some smart people there, their academic performance is not what one would call truly outstanding. What existed in most of the people who lived in Chichester, however, was a healthy dose of arrogance. As one might imagine, I had some trouble dealing with the difference in cultures.

As an example, during football practice one day, things got a little physical. This is a common event on a football field. Tempers flare and fights are not uncommon. I was playing safety and the play called for me to blitz the quarterback. When the ball was snapped, I charged through the line untouched and recorded my first organized football sack. It was a hard but clean hit. I put my face mask right into the shoulder pads of the quarterback, wrapped my arms around him and slammed him into the turf. I decided in that moment that I liked this game a lot.

As I reached out to help the quarterback up, a lineman came running over to me and blindsided me. I was dazed but realized I had been the victim of a cheap shot. I picked myself up and squared off against my attacker. A little pushing and shoving began and a circle of players formed around us. I recall one member of the group yelling to me, "Go ahead and hit him, I dare you. Then his father will sue your father for everything he's worth." I saw many other heads nod in affirmation, as if this was an acceptable way to solve the problem. I looked at my opponent who was nodding vigorously, saying, "Come on, let's go, my father will own your family."

I was so taken aback that I did not know what to do. I was simply standing there with my hands at my side, when the coaches finally separated us and sent me on a 30-lap journey around the practice field for fighting. As I ran around the field I kept looking at the players and wondering what planet they had come from. I was prepared to fight and they were prepared to sue. Something was wrong.

After getting injured several times, and given the problems I had on the team, I decided to quit. I liked to play sandlot baseball, so I thought maybe baseball players would be more in line with my kind of people. Wrong again. Having never played little league, or any other type of organized baseball, I quickly realized how far behind I was in terms of my skill level. While all the other players were basically sound in their mechanics and techniques, I was trying to learn how to shag fly balls, determine what a strike zone was, and how to read the signs from the third-base coach. While I could swear up a storm using my hands, I had no idea what the bunt sign was. I had a few moments in which I played well, but I was so far behind, I knew I would never really catch up. Moreover, a lot of the kids on the team also played football, so the problems remained.

I also had trouble in the classroom. My algebra skills were poor to begin with, and were compounded by the amount of time I missed by seeing Dr. Stephens. But I had to pass algebra to take geometry. Luckily, they gave me one year's credit for math, science, and English from Sleeping Giant. The graduation requirements were two years of math, two of science, and four years of English. This helped, but I was pretty far behind in those areas as well. Being the new kid, who is not a star athlete, who is not gifted academically, and who is not rich, does not usually put one in the fast track for popularity. Like most schools, the communication network was pretty extensive: word from my football colleagues traveled fast. Dan used to kid me about this in an attempt to make me feel better about my situation. He kept calling me a scholar-athlete. This was an award given each year to high school students around the state who excelled on the playing field as well as in the classroom. We still laugh at the irony of it all.

While social isolation was something I was used to, I had always gotten along with my colleagues. This did not happen in high school. Additionally, my teachers did not think highly of me—and that network is also a fast one. It was not long before I found teachers ignoring me, or treating me as if I were an idiot. A few even tried to ridicule me in class, although this did not happen that often. Nevertheless, the labeling effect took place and the derisive comments, though subtle, were apparent.

My reaction to the treatment by students and faculty was the same as it had always been: I became aggressive. I got into a lot of fights my first year there, although I was never caught by teachers or administrators. I was proud of the fact that I could defend myself and that I would not be hassled by anyone. I felt that if I had to endure my time in this school, at least I could do it in solitude and without the badgering that comes from being perceived as weak.

Moreover, the treatment I received by the teachers actually led me to believe that I was not smart, not talented, and should accept the fact that, as one teacher put it, "You will never go anywhere in life. The best you can hope for is to find a well-paying factory job somewhere. You do not have what it takes to go to college." I had a lot of respect for this teacher, at least until he said this to me. It was years later when I first learned about the labeling perspective of deviance that helped me understand what they were doing.

I used to spend a lot of time in the library reading anything to do with the police or with crime. I enjoyed the solitude and even avoided going to the cafeteria for lunch, preferring to find a study carrel in a corner of the library and eating lunch while reading a novel or a book on crime. It was here that I stumbled on the book, *The Police and the Public,* by Albert J.

Reiss [1970]. I admit I did not understand much of what he was saying, but I enjoyed reading the accounts by individual police officers. It would be years later that I would select him as the Chair of my dissertation committee at Yale. During that time, however, few knew about my love of reading and preferred to give me a label as a troublemaker and avoid me.

The Labeling Perspective

The essence of the labeling perspective is that deviance does not exist independent of the negative reaction of people who condemn it. Behaviors are never weird, bad, sick, or deviant in themselves. They are deviant only because someone or some group responds to them in this fashion. In his classic text, *The Outsiders*, Howard Becker [1964] states,

> deviance is not a quality of the act a person commits but
> rather a consequence of the application by others of rules
> and sanctions to an offender. The deviant is one to whom
> the label has successfully been applied; deviant behavior
> is behavior that people so label. [Becker 1964, p. 9]

Thus, labeling theory has a different focus from the variety of theoretical explanations of deviance or crime. Labeling theorists are not interested in the causal factors that lead an individual to commit a deviant or criminal act. Rather, labeling theory has pursued three interrelated concerns: the social historical development of deviant labels, the application of labels to certain types of people in specific times and places, and the symbolic and practical consequences of the labeling process.

During the 1960s, the writings of Howard Becker [1963], John Kitsuse [1962], Erving Goffman [1961, 1963], Kai Erikson [1966] and others set the stage for the development of this perspective. Moreover, the rise in popularity of the labeling theory and the emerging social climate was not accidental. Like many sociological contributions, the labeling perspective grew out of the massive changes that were taking place in American society. There were massive social and political struggles whose rumblings could be heard nationwide, especially on college campuses. The various protests and antiwar activists brought the label of deviance closer to home. All types of people were suddenly being arrested and treated like common criminals. Additionally, riots in the ghettos and incarceration for draft dodgers and conscientious objectors all had a profound effect on understanding the ways in which deviance comes to be defined in society.

According to the labeling perspective, the most crucial step in the development of a stable pattern of deviant behavior is usually the experience of being caught and publicly labeled deviant. Whether or not this happens to a person depends not so much on what the person does but on what other people do. Erikson [1962] expands on this a bit. He states:

> The community's decision to bring deviant sanctions against the individual... is a sharp rite of transition at once moving him out of his normal position in society and transferring him into a distinctive deviant role. The ceremonies which accomplish this change of status, ordinarily, have three related phases. They provide a formal confrontation between the deviant suspect and representatives of his community (as in the criminal trial or psychiatric case conference); they announce some judgment about the nature of his deviancy (a verdict or diagnosis for example); and they perform an act of social placement, assigning him to a special role (like that of a prisoner or patient) which redefines his position in society. [Erikson 1962, p. 3]

Once a person is stigmatized by being labeled a deviant, a self-fulfilling prophecy is initiated with others perceiving and responding to the person as a deviant. Further, once people are publicly processed as deviants, they are typically forced into a deviant group. And, as Lemert [1951] contends, once this happens the deviant will face an audience that anticipates the worst and will take steps to protect itself—which makes it difficult for the person to reintegrate him- or herself into society.

In summary, the labeling perspective has focused its attention on the societal attributes of those who react and those who are reacted against to explain why certain persons and not others are labeled as deviant. They argue that once a person has been labeled a deviant, and particularly if that person has passed through a *status degradation ceremony* [Garfinkel 1956] and forced to become a member of a deviant group, the person experiences a profound and often irreversible change. He or she has not only acquired an inferior status, he or she has developed a deviant self-image based upon the evaluations of him- or herself received through the action of others.

As you might imagine, the labeling process has profound consequences for individuals. Our society tends to be rather unforgiving in its treatment of deviants, irrespective of what they do to reintegrate themselves into society. And since we tend to be quick to affix labels, it is easy to see how problematic this can become for certain segments of our society.

Getting Tagged in High School

I was labeled and once it was applied, I had a difficult time having my behavior interpreted in any other way. In fact, it almost got me arrested and it did get me suspended. I had taken a creative writing class, largely because I had to fulfill a requirement and in part because I thought it might be interesting. I had always liked to write (I even wrote short stories from time to time) and I thought this would be a good chance to sharpen my writing skills. I discovered that the teacher, who was new to the school, had already heard about me from his colleagues. As such, I was already in trouble.

The requirements for the course were to submit couplets and other types of poetry to him for evaluation. He would then mark them as acceptable or in need of revisions. When the latter occurred, he would return the paper to the student and he or she would revise the poem and then resubmit it for consideration. There were a minimum number of papers that had to be accepted to earn a particular grade.

I quickly discovered that, while most of the other students' couplets and limericks were being accepted, mine were consistently returned for revisions. I began to suspect that I was being treated unfairly and as the term progressed, I began to worry about my grade. I could not graduate if I failed English and if my submissions were not accepted, that is exactly what would have happened. To test my suspicions, I decided to submit couplets and a few other forms from a Dan Folgelberg album. I literally plagiarized the segments of lyrics and submitted them as if they were my own. My reasoning was that if the artist could have the lyrics to his gold album accepted by the music company, that they were published, then my teacher should also accept them. If he accepted them, I would simply submit others so that they would not count. However, I was convinced they would be returned for revisions—I was right.

I waited until after class to discuss this with him, so that he would not lose face in front of the other students. He asked another student to stay after class and insisted that she remain present while we talked. I confronted him with this obvious case of discrimination and asked him to explain why he continued to make my life difficult. The discussion became heated, although he never denied the fact that he treated me differently than the other students. I became frustrated and told him that I could not graduate without passing English. He smiled and said that perhaps I was not ready to graduate and that another year or two here would better prepare me for life after high school. At this point, I became extremely angry and wondered aloud how cooperative he would be if he did not have the authority of the school behind him. He then terminated the conversation and told me that I would be suspended.

The next day I was called into the principal's office. I was met with the stern looks of the vice principal, the principal, and a police officer. The principal said that my teacher had accused me of threatening him "with great bodily injury" and that they were contemplating arresting me in addition to suspending me from school. It was clear that they had already made up their minds, but to give the impression of fairness, they asked me what had happened. I told them what had been happening and even produced the papers that he had marked. I also asked that they interview the student who was present at the time, but they refused to do so. Since my comments did not constitute the crime of threatening, they could not arrest me. The police officer left and I was told by the principal that I would be suspended for three weeks. Given that I had done nothing wrong, except to dispute the way in which the teacher was grading my papers, and that I had not violated any criminal laws, I asked why. The official charge was insubordination.

I tried to show them that the teacher was guilty of misrepresenting the situation to the administration and that they were negligent by failing to interview all the parties involved (I was thankful I had paid attention in my legal classes). As a result, I threatened to take my grievance to the board of education and to sue the school. It was a veiled threat because I realized that there was no way I could win. I did not come from a privileged background, my parents could not exert any influence over the situation, and the fact that I was innocent of any wrongdoing was immaterial.

The principal was more concerned with the morale of the faculty and dealing with this troublemaker than finding out what really happened. So I was suspended. As a parting shot, the principal intimated that I might not have been able to graduate because it was near the end of the school year and that I was close to violating the attendance policy. At that point I told him that if they kept me from graduating I would make a point of becoming one of the biggest problems in the history of the school. I would also make a point of calling the newspapers and writing editorials concerning the Gestapo-like tactics that the administration was using. It might not get me out any faster, but it would certainly bring an awful lot of problems to their desks. They recanted and allowed me to graduate, but the suspension still held. This is a good example of someone who has been labeled and cannot get a fair shake, even when he is innocent. It was a valuable lesson for me, one that I have never forgotten.

Living on My Own

After my sophomore year in high school, I decided that I wanted to earn some money. I had been reacquainted with Eddie and Dave, my old next-door neighbors from my first stint in Chichester. Eddie had registered for the same section of a Home Economics course as I did. We spent some time catching up on things and during the course of the marking period I discovered two things: I had a talent for cooking and that Eddie worked in a restaurant in town. He was able to get me a job as a dishwasher, and in the next two years I was to be promoted to cook and eventually to assistant manager. I started working only on weekend nights and this gradually increased to 40 hours per week by my junior year.

While working for the restaurant I got to know all the staff fairly well. One waitress, Sandy, became a close friend. She had a tough time growing up and was working two jobs in an attempt to get out of debt. In 1978, Sandy moved to St. Louis. Before leaving she offered me her apartment. Her living situation was an informal one with the landlord. There were 12 apartments in her building and the only way someone could move in was to have the recommendation of a previous tenant. The rent for the three-room apartment, without utilities, was a staggering $75 per month.

Since I was working full-time, I would have no trouble making the payments. I calculated my expenses and how much I earned and went to Dan. I knew he could get into a lot of trouble if the state found out I had moved into my own apartment. I was still a minor, although I would turn 18 in November, three months away. He agreed and before I knew it, I was a high school senior with my own apartment. It did not take long for people to realize that there was a private place to go. Suddenly, I had lots of friends. While I had maintained a distant relationship with many of them, now they wanted to be my closest companion.

I spent a lot of time working at the restaurant. Given that my teachers expected little of me and I was happy to oblige them, my grades were not up to par. In fact, while I had made the honor roll a couple of times, just to prove a point, for the most part, I hovered just below the minimum requirement for graduation. I had no respect for the school, the teachers, or the students. They were elitist snobs and I wanted no part of them. There were a few exceptional teachers, both in terms of their talent as well as their understanding of human dignity. I latched on to them and tried to learn as much as I could from them.

One of these people was a teacher who taught courses on the legal system. He suffered from polio as a child and wore braces on his legs. He was exceptionally bright and took an interest in me. I learned later that he was attracted to what can be called "nonconventional" students: ones who did not necessarily fit into the Chichester mold. Most of his students were targeted in the noncollege track and spent much of their time in shop classes, study halls, or more commonly, the principal's office. He treated me with respect and never talked down to me. I still have a great deal of regard for him, largely because he was more intelligent and affluent than the vast majority of the people who worked in the school, yet he detested arrogance in people. In short, he was comfortable with who he was and was successful enough not to have to tell people about it. He inspired my interest in the law and for that I will always be grateful.

Another person who had a positive impact on me was my English teacher. She had a reputation for being difficult and lived up to it. She recognized my limitations as a writer, but instead of being mean-spirited and caustic, she was constructive and nurturing. She once called me "a diamond in the rough." I did not know what it meant at the time, and like a good English teacher, she told me to go to the library and find out.

When I was a graduating senior I watched her refuse several students who had asked her to sign their year book (while she was tough, the smart students used to flock to her). After observing this, I thought she would do the same to me. As I was walking down the hall one day, however, she sought me out and told me how proud she was of my progress and that I had matured as a writer in a short period of time. Then she took the yearbook out of my hand and signed it. Her inscription read: "To Bob McNamara, a diamond in the rough." To this day, I remember how good it felt to hear her say she was proud of me.

While I became accustomed to my new home, the Hartmanns sold their condo in Chichester and moved to a new home in North Haven. I still went there for holidays or to attend Leslie's and Tracy's school activities. I wanted to be around to watch them grow up and vowed that I would do the same for the newest addition to the family, A. J. My involvement continues to this day. Whenever Kristy and I are in town, we stay part of the time with them and try to keep up to date with what is going on the their lives. We do not see each other as much as we would like to, but when we do, we simply pick up where we left off.

Finding My Way

Life on my own was not exactly easy. I worked a lot and had little time for social activities. I had my share of girlfriends and other associates, but I had come to be a loner and preferred it that way. At the end of my senior year, I left the restaurant and began working at various jobs. I had been awarded Social Security survivorship benefits when my father died, and when I reached 18 years of age, I was eligible to start receiving the payments. I had no real emotions when he died, largely because I did not know him. And what I did remember, I did not like much. I had seen him once before he died, and it was obvious he had not changed. He still drank to excess, worked sporadically, and generally spent most of his time in bars.

The benefits allowed me to spend some time trying to figure out who I was and what I wanted to be. I had always wanted to be a cop, but for some reason I did not pursue this career right away. I had started taking courses at a community college nearby, but at about the same time, I had become involved in a long-distance relationship. Her name was Lisa and she lived in San Diego, California. The two things were somewhat incompatible for me. Like most people involved in a relationship, I wanted to be in San Diego and spend my time there. I had visited her once during high school and for a while I thought I wanted to live there. So much so that I actually sold all my possessions, gave my apartment away to someone else, and flew out there. I stayed at the YMCA in the downtown section of the city for about two weeks and realized that I had made a terrible mistake.

I called the Hartmanns and asked if I could stay with them until I found another place to stay. I felt a little strange in asking them: after all, their obligation to me officially ended when I turned 18. They did not have to welcome me back into their home, and if they refused, I would have understood. Once again they saved me from disaster. I stayed with them for about six months, when I began working for a fast food chain.

The owners were young and full of energy and had lots of room in their organization for me to grow. I quickly became a key person in the organization and, as I mentioned in a previous chapter, it was not long before I decided to return to school to study law and criminal justice. Again, the Hartmanns gave me the chance to be a somewhat typical adolescent and young adult, with the opportunity to grow a little and try to figure out what path in life I wanted to take. Without their encouragement and support, these pages would never have been written. In the next chapter, I will explore the impact of role models not just in situations like mine, but in all types of situations. The research on this subject seems fairly clear and its implications for social policy are far reaching.

References

Anastasi, A. (1988). *Psychological testing* (6th ed.). New York: Macmillan.

Becker, H. (Ed.). (1964). *The other side*. New York: The Free Press.

Becker, H. (1963). *Outsiders*. New York: The Free Press.

Erikson, K. (1966). *Wayward Puritans*. New York: MacMillan.

Erikson, K. (1962). Notes on the sociology of deviance. In H. Becker (Ed.), *The other side* (pp. 2-15). Chicago: University of Chicago Press.

Garfinkel, H. (1956). Conditions of successful degradation ceremonies. *American Journal of Sociology, 61*, 420-424.

Goffman, E. (1963). *Stigma: Notes on the management of a spoiled identity.* New York: Simon and Schuster.

Goffman, E. (1961). *Asylums: Essays on the social situation of mental patients and other inmates*. New York: Anchor.

Kitsuse, J. (1962). Societal reaction to deviance: Problems of theory and method. *Social Problems, 9*, 247-256.

Lemert, E. (1951). *Social pathology*. New York: McGraw-Hill.

Murphy, K. R., & Davidshofer, C. O. (1991). *Psychological testing* (2nd ed.). Englewood Cliffs, NJ: Prentice-Hall.

Reiss, A. J. (1970). *The police and the public*. New Haven, CT: Yale University Press.

Further Readings on Deviance

Conrad, P., & Schneider, J. W. (1980). *Deviance and medicalization: From madness to sickness.* St. Louis, MO: C.V. Mosby.

Gibbs, J. (1966). Conceptions of deviant behavior: The old and the new. *Pacific Sociological Review, 9,* 9-14.

Gove, W. (Ed.). (1975). *The labeling of deviance.* New York: John Wiley.

Gusfield, J. (1966). *Symbolic crusade: Status, politics and the American temperance movement.* Chicago, IL: University of Illinois Press.

Mankoff, M. (1971). Societal reaction and career deviance: A critical analysis. *Sociological Quarterly, 12*(2), 204-217.

Mead, G. H. (1928). The psychology of punitive justice. *American Journal of Sociology, 23,* 577-602.

Schur, E. (1971). *Labeling deviant behavior: Its sociological implications.* New York: Harper Row.

Smith, R. T. (1975). Societal reaction and physical disability: Contrasting perspectives. In W. Gove (Ed.), *The labeling of deviance* (pp. 147-156). New York: John Wiley and Sons.

Tannenbaum, F. (1938). *Crime and the community.* New York: McGraw-Hill.

Final Thoughts

By no means is this the end of the story. I have come a long way in a relatively short period of time and there are many things I still want to accomplish. And while I do not think we can ever isolate ourselves from the past, I am trying to let the negative and painful memories fade. In many ways, I think I am only now learning how and why certain things are important to me. For a long time I did not have time to ponder the way I felt: I was too busy surviving. Today I am trying to work through some of the lingering baggage.

Music, Holidays, and Memories

For instance, recently the music of the 1970s has become fashionable. I have many friends who think this was an exciting era and the music is both upbeat and inspiring. In fact, many bars offer "70s nights," where the music of this decade is the focus of attention. Thus, while many enjoy the "oldies," a term used by my students (one I struggle to accept), it evokes many painful memories. I used music as a means of escaping much of what was happening to me at the time. I remember sitting on my bed in the Douglass home for hours listening to the songs of the group Chicago on an old eight-track tape player I salvaged from the trash bin. In other homes, I would try to imagine being somewhere else while listening to Donna Summer, Billy Joel, Aerosmith, Manford Man, the Beach Boys, the

Doobie Brothers, or James Taylor. For those moments I was able to escape the emotional stress of my living situation.

To hear those songs today, however, brings back many of those painful memories. Thus, while many of my friends happily dance to the songs of the 1970s, or buy the CDs offered on television as the "songs of the decade," I struggle to share their enthusiasm. In fact, it sometimes depresses me to hear this music. When most people hear old songs, they remember where they were and what they were doing when the song was released. I was the same way, except few of my memories were happy ones. For instance, when I was living at City Point with my father and the situation had reached its lowest point, just after he tried to choke me, I recall hearing the song "Have You Seen Her" by the Chi-Lites for the first time. I remember sitting on a park bench near the Albie Booth Boy's Club watching some of the older kids playing basketball nearby and heard it playing on their radio. It made me sad and to this day, when I hear it, I find myself switching stations. Similarly, there is a song from the 1960s entitled "Whiter Shade of Pale" by Procul Harem. It has a distinctive introduction and I feel my stomach begin to tighten each time I hear it.

As difficult as it is, I am trying to work through those painful thoughts. A few years ago, Leslie and her husband Scott bought tickets to a Crosby, Stills, and Nash concert in New Haven and invited Kristy and me to go with them. It was a warm summer evening, the band played some of their biggest hits, and I had a great time. I do not get to see Leslie that often these days and I really enjoyed spending time with her. Even now when I hear one of those songs, I find myself substituting the painful thoughts of the past with those of her and that evening.

This past year, on a recent trip home, Tracy was able to secure tickets to a '70s Revival concert for Leslie, Scott, Dan, and me. Initially, I thought that this would be a bad idea and it would bring back too many memories, but I did not want to hurt my sister's feelings either. As it turned out, it was really a lot of fun. It was amusing to watch K.C. and the Sunshine Band, especially the lead singer, now well into his forties, try to dance as he did in years past. It was hilarious. This too, becomes another substitution of happy memories for the old ones.

Holidays are still a problem however. For years, especially when I worked as a regional manager for the fast food chain, as often as possible, I would give some of my employees the holidays off and work in one of the stores myself. I know holidays are an especially depressing time for some people, but for me, it is particularly troublesome. This was true even though many of those years have been spent with the Hartmanns. To this day we spend Christmas day together, but I always get into a "funk" around this time of year.

This also happens at Thanksgiving. I have a great deal to be thankful for and I am grateful for everything I have been given. Still, I find myself occasionally putting up those emotional shields that prevent me from really enjoying the holidays. Part of the reason may be traced to my memories of when I was living on the streets and peering into the homes of families. I used to wonder what life must be like for them. But Thanksgiving is supposed to be a day of happiness, right?

As an added bonus, my birthday usually falls on or near Thanksgiving. And it occurs at a time in my life when I have two families that are excited about it: the Hartmanns and Kristy's family. I have not included much about them in this story, but they are important to me. They accepted me into their family and made me feel as though I belonged. They are a special group of people and they have helped me to achieve the kind of emotional stability that allows me to talk candidly about my past. Thus, despite some evidence of positive memories and experiences, the emotional scars remain. I continue to try to work through it; however, it is not easy and I have needed a lot of help along the way.

On Therapy and Therapists

Some might be ashamed to admit seeking therapy to deal with their problems, especially a male in our society. I am sure my father would not think a "shrink" would do anything to help me solve my problems, but I disagree. But to be honest, for a long time I never gave much thought to therapy and in some ways I remain skeptical. My training and experiences with psychologists and psychiatrists have not inspired confidence in their ability to resolve problems for people. Having said that, however, I think there is a great value in talking to someone about one's emotional issues. In fact, when people talk to friends about a problem, they are engaging in a form of therapy. And essentially, that is what I am doing now. I find that I can organize my thoughts and feelings about things by verbalizing them and writing them down. The real value of therapy then, it seems to me, is to have someone who knows how to get the person to understand and confront her or his problems, and to be able to understand their complexities. This is especially true when trying to unpack the mystery of how people cope and adapt to their problems.

I have always been adept at channeling my negative energy. For instance, when I was in college and had a problem or something stressful was going on, I would throw myself into my studies. It was a great problem solver, because school took so much time and energy and my efforts yielded results: I received high marks and progressed to the graduate level of study. It also opened the door to job opportunities. Even today, I find myself slipping into that mode. When things get painful, or I get into one of my "funks," I immerse myself in my courses or my research. And of course, the result is the same: I publish a book, an article, or some other tangible sign of professional success. This is not to say that dedication or ambition has little value. Rather, what I am saying is that for me, my ability to focus and block out everything else has always been a tremendously successful coping strategy when other problems in my life emerge. And while it may have been necessary for me to employ that technique at one time, I now know that the consequence of this strategy is that I miss out on a lot of things. It also means that it is time to put it away and find another method. This is difficult, since this has been the only way I know and it has proven to be successful time and time again.

Upon reflection, it seems to me that in many ways, my experiences and situations taught me how to adapt or cope with adversity. Unfortunately, at times I think it has taught me too well. For instance, while I grew up in bars and learned a lot about the things that occur there, most of my experiences have been negative ones. As a child, I saw how fights could break out at a moment's notice, seemingly without provocation. I would also feel the effects of what happened in bars when my father would lose a bet, get drunk, come home, and slap me around out of frustration.

Additionally, when I worked in private security, I was usually the one who would be required to break up the fights in bars, night clubs, parks, emergency rooms. Thus, in many ways I do not think I ever learned to enjoy or appreciate the comraderie or the fun associated with night life.

I have similar feelings about alcohol. I drink sparingly because of the deleterious effects it has on the body, but I also think that there are two other reasons, both of which are related, why I shy away from it. I feel the need to be careful about drinking because I have many examples in my family of abusing alcohol (especially my paternal uncles). In some ways I think they serve as an example of what I do *not* want to be. As a result, I have gone in the opposite direction and chosen not to drink, or to carefully monitor myself. Parenthetically, perhaps this also explains my general approach to life. While my father and his family lacked a strong work ethic, my grandfather, who spent his entire life practicing self-discipline, did. And, while it is only speculation on my part, I saw how little we had doing it my father's way and how much my grandfather obtained through hard work and determination.

The second reason has more to do with my personality. Recall that during the time I was involved in a gang, my nickname was One Speed. This was given to me because, whatever the task or activity, I pursued it with a single-minded determination until I achieved my goal. As I mentioned in an earlier chapter, this approach to life has remained constant: I still pursue my objectives and leisure activities with a sort of reckless abandon. Some might say this is indicative of an addictive personality and maybe there is some truth to that. Others might simply call it Irish stubbornness. Of course, I am not qualified to make that kind of assessment, but I do think it has a lot to do with my attitude toward drinking. In sum, because of a long history of alcoholism in my family, and because of this approach to life, I need to be careful about the things I allow myself to do. A good illustration is my recent involvement in ice hockey.

Hockey Boy

In the winter of 1974, I was living on the farm with the Crosses. At that time, I decided I wanted to learn how to ice skate. One of the neighbors nearby had a pond and each winter all the kids in the area would meet to play hockey. By this time, I was searching for any reason to get out of the house and hockey seemed to be the kind of sport I would like: it was fast, it involved hitting people, and it looked like a lot of fun. I set out to learn on my own, since no one in the Cross family could or would teach me. I found a small area on the Cross's property that had sufficiently frozen and was large enough to move around. It was not a pond by any means, it was more like a marsh, with twigs and weeds growing above the ice line.

I spent the better part of two afternoons with a shovel trying to cut down the weeds and twigs to create a clear area on which to skate. The Crosses watched me with amusement and laughed at me when I told them I would teach myself. While I had no idea how well I would do, I did take a book out of the school library on playing hockey. It was written by Gordie Howe, one of the best players in the history of the game. I poured over the chapters about skating, especially maneuvering and skating backwards. It did not sound difficult, so I flipped ahead to the chapters on shooting, conditioning, and buying equipment. The more I read, I found I really liked the game. The fact that it is one of the most expensive sports to play never occurred to me.

The first day was a disaster. I had already found an old pair of hockey skates in the barn and discovered that they fit properly. I was ready to become a hockey player. That afternoon when I arrived home from school, the temperature was about 20° Fahrenheit. By the time I changed clothes and laced up my skates, it was about 10° without accounting for the wind-chill factor.

I quickly realized that my ankles were not strong enough to support my weight. They were at 45-degree angles to the blades of the skates. I fell a lot: my hips became sore, my elbows and knees took a beating from hitting the ice so frequently, not to mention I was sweating and freezing at the same time. It took all my concentration to simply remain upright. I finally gave up for the day when the sun set and it became dark. The next morning I could barely walk, but by the afternoon, I was back out on my skates. Day after day I practiced and eventually I became proficient at skating. Each night the Crosses would laugh at me and call me Bobby Orr, after the famous player for the Boston Bruins. With each passing day, I was able to perform the way Gordie Howe had written about: he was a good teacher and I learned a lot. In fact, I became so good that after only about two weeks, I wanted to try skating at the large pond nearby.

After a few outings there, and a couple of nasty spills, I could actually hold my own with the other kids. From there, I wanted to go to a skating rink. One of the guys in the neighborhood played on a hockey team and I used to watch him practice at the local rink. Some times he would go to public skating, and after a while, I began to accompany him. I desperately wanted to play hockey, but could not afford the equipment. Not to mention, being a good skater is one thing, being a good hockey player is another.

In July 1974, after I left the Crosses' home and moved in with Mrs. Douglass, I scraped together enough money to buy a pair of "real" hockey skates. It was one of my happiest times. Every Friday night I would attend public skating sessions at the local rink. Sometimes James would come along, and other times it would be our next door neighbor, Frankie. He and I became good friends and he also liked to skate, though not as much as I did. Other times, I would simply go alone. I really enjoyed the freedom it gave me. This pattern continued when I moved in with the Hartmanns. In fact, I went to the Chichester rink so frequently that the staff hired me as a skating monitor on the weekends. It was free ice time and they even gave me a hamburger or two. I was happy just to be able to skate for free.

To this day I enjoy skating. While hockey is not exactly a popular sport in South Carolina, I recently had the chance to go skating with one of my colleagues from Furman. He is originally from upstate New York and plays in a hockey league. After my second time with him, I was again hooked. I now look forward to the days when I can return to one of the most enjoyable activities I have ever known. Moreover, there are "pick-up" hockey games during the week and I have started to play. As I skate around, having the time of my life, I can still recall some of the lessons from Gordie Howe's book. I think it is ironic that I lived in New England my entire life and never played the game (largely because I could not afford to), only to come to the South, where it is not exactly the most popular sport, and begin playing in earnest. Another twist of irony occurred when the manager of the rink offered me a job as a skate guard/Zamboni operator. Like the last time, money was not the motivating factor in this decision: rather it is love of the activity (and of course the free ice time).

Reading Really Is Fundamental

During the period in which I taught myself how to skate, I realized that there were no limits to the number of things I could learn. For every activity, there is a book that has been written about it. I thought that if I could somehow acquire the book, there was nothing in the world I could not understand. This was an important lesson for me. I may not be an expert, but, as Gordie Howe showed me, I can learn from one by what he or she has written.

This love of reading is probably the one thing that allowed me to keep my sanity during those trying years. Reading allows me to learn, but it also provides me with a way to escape. When I was younger, I could forget all my problems and lose myself in a good book. Even today, as my wife will attest, when things become stressful or hectic, she can usually find me in a corner somewhere with a good novel. Just as I did long ago, I can lose myself completely in the story and forget whatever was happening around me. Unfortunately, not everyone has the chance to enjoy this wonderful past time.

According to some experts, literacy is considered to be the ability to read and write at the eighth-grade level [Smith 1995]. By one account, it is estimated that approximately 23 million Americans are illiterate [Segal 1992]. This number may be low, however. According to Kozol [1985], an estimated 25 million American adults cannot read a letter from their child's teacher or the front page of a daily paper. Moreover, another 35 million are barely able to read at a level that allows them to survive in our society. Collectively, these 60 million people are about a third of the entire adult population. This problem is particularly relevant in the workplace.

Smith [1995] contends that 65% of the American workforce currently reads below a ninth-grade level. The problem of illiteracy is underscored by the fact that at least 70% of on-the-job reading material, including safety information, is written at a range from the ninth-grade to college-level aptitude. While extensive research has been conducted on the problems of illiteracy, the clearest finding is that the problem is serious and increasing. Thus, not only are many people prevented from navigating the social and physical landscape, they do not have the ability to engage in one of life's most wondrous pleasures.

Where Is Everyone?

As I mentioned earlier, my grandfather passed away a few years ago of prostate cancer. He was 98 years old. Now that I own my own home, struggle with fertilizer and grass seed, and consider starting a garden in the spring, I find myself thinking about him a lot lately, especially when I water the lawn. My father died when I was 17, in 1977. The cause of death was aspiration. This occurs when a person attempts to vomit, but for some reason is unable to expel the material, which results in death due to asphyxiation. As the story was related to me, one night my father was drunk and unconscious. He began to vomit, aspirated, and did not recover.

Brad lives in Connecticut and holds a management position in the federal government. He holds a Bachelor's Degree in Business and lives with his wife, his in-laws, and a terrific golden retriever named Mollie, in a large home on about 12 acres of land. I believe he is living the American Dream. The same is true of my brother Mark. Married, with one child, he is a civil engineer with a specialization in nuclear energy. He is successful, happy, and recently completed the requirements for a Master's Degree. I am proud of both of them. Like me, they have worked hard to succeed, and had a lot of help along the way.

Daryl is another story. His whereabouts are unknown. The last time I talked to him, in 1989, he was an aspiring Ku Klux Klansman. Daryl used to work as a dog trainer and wanted to provide his new brethren with attack training for their animals. About a year later, when his relationship with the Klan did not seem to be working out, Mark and I loaned him some money to become a semi-owner/operator in a tractor trailer business. Since then, no one has heard from him. Given his propensity for violence and trouble, there is a good possibility that he is either dead or in prison. Unfortunately, his may be the most tragic of stories in this family.

After a failed marriage in 1988, Daryl moved to Florida and stayed with my mother. As he put it, he was going to play upon her guilt for abandoning us. They had a falling out a short time later, ending the relationship completely. For a time he was living with a woman and her son across the street from my mother's trailer park. Periodically she would see him in passing but refused to speak to him. Daryl maintained some contact with his three brothers, primarily Mark, but a few years ago Mark changed telephone numbers and lost contact with him. For a while Mark tried to get in touch with him through my mother, but she refused to pass along any messages. Since then no one has heard from him.

I recently attended a conference in Mobile, Alabama. I realized that the town he was last known to be living in was only an hour's drive away. Kristy and I visited the town's court house, police department, utility companies, even the tax collector. According to their records, Daryl owns no property, has no vehicle registered, does not have an account with the utility companies, and has not been arrested.

While it is possible that he is living with someone who pays the bills and owns the vehicles, which would not be all that surprising, it is unlikely that he is still living in the area.

We were able to access a 1990 police report that showed he was involved in a domestic dispute with my mother and her husband. We found the address only to discover from a resident in the area that the street names and numbers had been changed around 1991. Thus, even if we had the correct address, which is an assumption, when the city changed some of the street names and renumbered the homes, our hopes of finding him diminished.

I even tried to contact some of the surrounding towns, including Mobile, to see if he moved a short distance away. Unfortunately, I was unsuccessful. At this point, it is hard to know exactly what has happened to him. I even tried to locate him through the post office, but was unsuccessful there as well. According to the letter carrier who worked in the area, Daryl's last known address was in a transient neighborhood. I simply do not think he is in the area. He could be in another part of Florida or any other state, for that matter. As a last resort, I have sent requests to the Bureau of Vital Statistics in Tallahassee to see if he is listed on any death certificates.

On the drive back to Mobile that day, I thought a lot about him. What he was doing, where he was living, what his life was like. I remembered that Daryl used to keep all his possessions in a plastic laundry basket. That way, if he had to leave, packing a suitcase was never a problem. While I was not surprised that we failed to locate him, I did become conscious of my own success and wondered why his life was so different from mine. Recently, I hired a private investigator and contacted a few friends in the law enforcement community to find him. As of this writing we have not been successful.

As I mentioned, my mother still lives in Florida with her ex-boss. They married some years ago and own a trailer park in the northern part of the state. She keeps in touch with Brad, and occasionally, with Mark. She calls them on their birthdays, Thanksgiving, and sometimes at Christmas. She is close to retirement and thinks she is going to buy a recreational vehicle and travel with her husband.

The only contact I have had with her was at my grandfather's funeral. I did not plan to attend, but did so out of respect for him. All his children were there, and she made a big deal out of my presence, almost as if to show everyone that her boys still loved her. It was a shallow attempt at best and I do not think she fooled anyone. Prior to this I had only one meeting with her, which was at my request.

I wanted to hear her side of the story about what had happened to me, which I will describe in greater detail below. I currently do not maintain any contact with her, nor do I want to. In my mind, when she left she relinquished any rights or privileges as a parent. I have two parents now and they have done more for me than anyone I have ever known.

   If there is one thing that I would want from my biological mother, it would be what few mementos that were collected during my childhood. I have few pictures of myself as a young boy and what I was able to acquire were given to me by Brad and his wife from their photo albums. Mark once told me that my mother has an entire collection of memorabilia, including a few awards I won while in grammar school. At times I have given some thought to asking her to borrow them so that I might make copies, but decided against it. I would like them to show my future children what their father looked like when he was a boy. Perhaps some day I will ask her for them, but I would not be at all surprised if she refused my requests.

Protest and Denial

In 1991, I sat down with her and had a long talk about what had happened. She was visiting her husband's mother in Connecticut and we arranged to meet. By this time, I had gained access to my file with the Department of Child and Families and confronted her with the evidence contained in the dossier. She simply denied any wrongdoing and began to show me the canceled checks that she had kept for the four years I was in the care of others. To her, these checks represented her responsibility as a parent. She showed me check after check, made out to so many different people I lost count, to prove that she took care of me. At one point, I realized that not only was she in a healthy state of denial, but I also suspected that perhaps the mental disorders my grandfather had suffered from had been passed down to the next generation. In many ways, I felt sorry for her. Deep down, however, I think she knew what she did. I think she became too tired to take care me and wanted a different life. Then she met her present husband and suddenly that became a possibility. This was especially true when the State of Connecticut agreed to assume responsibility for my care.

   Thus, while I think she is delusional, at some level, I think she knows what she has done and feels guilty about it at times. Daryl provided some support for this conclusion. When he first moved in with her, they had a number of in-depth conversations about life, the family, and what had happened. In those conversations she intimated to him that she had made two mistakes in her life: marrying my father and abandoning me. If what Daryl said is true, this is evidence of her understanding the implications of what she had done. Despite the fact that everything turned out okay, the odds of success were overwhelmingly against me. By all rights, I should not be writing this book, or have a Ph.D. from Yale University. I beat the odds, but not on my own and not without a great deal of luck.

What made me so fortunate? I honestly do not know. Perhaps it was my ability to recognize the difference between right and wrong, perhaps it was my ability to "read" people well. And perhaps it was the Irish stubbornness that made me left-handed: that I would not submit to other people's wishes/demands. Maybe it was a combination of all three things. Nevertheless, I could never be where I am today without being given the opportunity and the emotional support to succeed.

The Influence of Role Models

As I mentioned, while living with the Hartmanns, when I worked at the restaurant in Chichester, there were many nights when I would not arrive home until late in the evening. This was especially true on Friday and Saturdays, when the restaurant did not close until one in the morning. Typically, when I came home I could not sleep and stayed up until early in the morning watching old movies in the downstairs den. This area was not insulated and it was rather cold at night. As such, I would bring a blanket downstairs with me, perhaps a snack, and then watch an old John Wayne movie until I was tired enough to finally go to sleep. One night, Leslie waited for me to return and then wanted to watch the movie with me. I was touched. I also felt a little guilty that I was depriving a child of her rest. There were many times when I tried to get her to return to bed, not because I did not enjoy her company, which I did, but because I did not want her to be exhausted the next day.

This became our little ritual: we would go downstairs and watch the movie together while covering ourselves with a blanket. This may be speculation on my part, but as I write this I realize that perhaps she enjoyed this as much as I used to enjoy my time alone with Mark and Brad when *they* came home late from work and watched the late movie. Years later, when Leslie was a senior in high school, she was required to write a personal statement as part of her college application. She chose to write about me. It was flattering and meant a lot to me. As a graduation gift that year, I gave her perhaps the most significant thing I owned at the time, a book entitled, *Ordeal by Sea*, which is an account of what happened to the U.S.S. Indianapolis during World War II.

At one time, I became a real student of this era. When our fourth-grade class at Horace Day School walked several blocks to the Davenport Library, I went immediately into the corner that had books on the second world war. I read books on the Flying Tigers fighter squadron, stories of infantrymen on Iwo Jima, the battle over Britain, everything I could find. It was a small library, but it was an oasis to me. I could go there and hide in a corner and read. Sometimes I would get so engrossed in the stories that I would not hear my teacher calling us together to walk back to school. Thus, while the other kids sat around and had the stories read to them by the librarian, I snuck away and read on my own. I suspect my teacher knew where I was, but was kind enough to allow me the chance to explore. After all, how many times can a kid ask to use the restroom and never return before the teacher realized what was happening? I am forever grateful that she allowed a small boy the chance to explore.

As part of her graduation gift, I took Leslie on a tour of my old neighborhoods, especially the Davenport Library. I tried to explain to her what had happened to me, but even then it was too painful. I wanted her to realize the opportunities she had been given and to see why the book was so important to me. I had stolen it out of the library one day and kept it for about ten years before giving it to her. Through that time, I read and reread the story, often because it was the only book I had that I could call my own. It meant a lot to me to be able to give it to her, but it also meant a lot that she held me in such high regard. I was her older brother and she respected me. I do not know if I was a role model (in some ways I hope that I was not), but it does bring up the issue of the influence a person like this can have on another.

Research on Role Models

The idea of the role model has been an important part of sociological thought. In his classic essays on the concept of the reference group, Merton [1968] states,

> Multiple roles are adopted for emulation rather than emulation remaining confined to the one role on the basis of which the initial psychological relationship was established. Just as roles can be segregated from one another in the course of social interaction, so they can be in the form of reference orientations. Emulation of a peer, a parent or a public figure may be usefully described as adoption of a role model. [Merton 1968, pp. 356-7]

It seems fairly clear that mentors or role models, especially for young adults, are an important factor in shaping their attitudes, values, and beliefs, as well as their behavior. And this relationship can influence the child in both positive and negative ways.

A great deal of the sociological research on the influence of role models focuses on teenagers and issues relating to poverty, race, education, physical environment, pregnancy, employment, and violence (see Greene [1993]; Mayer and Jencks [1989]; Anderson [1991]; Duneier [1992]; and Wilson [1987]).

For instance, in the 1980s perhaps the most prominent explanation for inner-city problems emphasized the increased levels of poverty in poor neighborhoods. The main thrust of this explanation was the shift in the economy, specifically the tendency for factory jobs to move out of the city and to areas where costs of production were cheaper. In perhaps the most influential work on the subject, William Julius Wilson [1987] focuses on the large numbers of working- and middle-class blacks moving from the inner city, which exacerbates the social isolation of those that are forced to remain. Thus, the problems of a changing economy has led to an increase in residential segregation for the poor. Wilson also argues that the departure of working and middle class African Americans from cities also leads to a decline in the number and quality of role models. This further intensifies the problems in the inner city.

The impact of Wilson's work essentially set the stage for research on poverty into the 1990s. The focus of attention was directed toward the issue of segregation within certain zones of the city, however, not on the significance of middle-class role models. While the assertions made by Wilson seemed logical, that the middle-class people who left the inner city had been an important part of neighborhood life, there was scant evidence to document this generally held belief.

One study of this demographic shift, as well as an examination of the effects of role models in urban neighborhoods, is found in Anderson's [1991] work in Philadelphia. In echoing Wilson's earlier point, this study attempted to identify what had been lost by the departure of many middle- and working-class African Americans. Anderson argues that these groups served the community as visible symbols of "success, and moral value, living examples of the fruits of hard work, perseverance, decency and propriety" [Anderson 1991, p. 58]. Thus, he argues that the people who left the inner city "were effective, meaningful role models lending the community a certain moral integrity" [p. 59].

Anderson underscores this point with his discussion of the increase in teenage pregnancy. He argues that the number of traditional adult female role models, who often exerted a considerable amount of social control over their younger counterparts, lost much of their ability to influence young women. This is due largely to the deterioration of inner city neighborhoods, which are characterized by the infestation of drugs and dealers, prostitutes, and violence. In this type of environment, Anderson argues that even the adult role models have been taxed to the breaking point: they too have become demoralized and many have left these neighborhoods, or, as he states, "some succumb to the street" [Anderson in Jencks & Peterson 1991, p. 382].

The same is true with employment. As the number of jobs in the inner city have dwindled, the opportunities for young African American men have decreased as well. As meaningful jobs become increasingly scarce, the traditional male role models, who emphasize the importance of hard work, determination, and a belief in the American Dream, become irrelevant, largely because they are no longer possible. Thus, while some will remain and continue to attempt to have a positive influence on the next generation, many have decided the conditions in these neighborhoods have reached an unacceptable level. Like their female counterparts, these "old heads" typically move out of the area. In their wake a new role model does emerge, however—one that is involved in criminal activity, typically the drug trade [Anderson, in Jencks & Peterson 1991].

In contrast to Wilson and Anderson, Duneier [1992] questions the argument that the departure of "significant and meaningful" role models implies that the people who remain in the inner city are inadequate role models or are incapable of having a significant impact on the members of the community. He asserts that this type of observation continues to perpetuate stereotypes of people who live in inner city environments. He states,

> Part of the problem with the role model explanation is that it follows from the sociological discipline's oversimplified images of the urban ghettos as significantly cut off from the rest of American society. Wilson introduced the term "social isolation" to describe the lack of ghetto contact with mainstream culture, and it has since been picked up by the mass media. But, as Christopher Jencks has illustrated, the idea fails to acknowledge the extent to which the problems of ghetto life reflect broader trends in the wider society. [Duneier 1992, p. 127]

Moreover, Duneier argues that it is erroneous to assume that, as many sociologists and others have contended, the absence of middle-class African Americans means there are no role models within the working or poor classes.

In short, Duneier is critical of sociologists who often create the impression that without middle-class or even upper working-class African Americans, the community has no moral base. It is not that middle-class people do not have a significant role to play in the life of the inner city. Rather, this picture demeans the working-class role models who do exist there, and the attention given only to middle- and upper middle-class individuals implies that they are crucial to the survival of these communities.

What Have We Learned?

There can be little doubt that the demographic shift has resulted in serious problems for the poor in the inner city. And while the debate concerning the significance of middle- and upper-class African Americans as role models continues, there can be little doubt that positive, constructive role models, especially for inner city adolescents, are desperately needed.

It also seems obvious that most of the research on the subject calls attention to the importance of having a positive influence on young persons, which, in turn, shapes their outlook on life, their confidence, and their belief in themselves. There are success stories, even in the worst of neighborhoods, where young adults who should have succumbed to the street did not. They were somehow able to resist the temptations of unacceptable behavior such as crime, gang life, and drug use, and to somehow square their self-images with those of their peers. In virtually all of these instances, there was someone who was instrumental in putting and keeping them on the right path (see Williams and Kornblum [1994]). Thus, it seems that the task is to provide more positive role models and to increase their influence, while eliminating (if possible) the negative ones.

For those individuals who serve as role models for inner city youth, such as professional athletes, the importance of their public behavior cannot be underscored enough. Recently, Charles Barkley, a professional basketball player for the Houston Rockets, publicly stated that he was not a role model and did not wish to be one. He felt that he did not want the responsibility of having his behavior scrutinized by millions of people. His statement included words to the effect of "I am who I am and I don't want people expecting me to be nice all the time." Sorry, Mr. Barkley, but whether you like it or not, whether you want this role or not, you are a role model to millions of children and your behavior *does* serve as an example of appropriate (and inappropriate) behavior. That this man, who makes millions of dollars each year, who gladly accepts the notoriety and prestige (not to mention endorsement contracts) his position accords him in our society, can simply shirk his social responsibilities as a public figure is unconscionable, and he is naive to think that his attitudes and behaviors are not emulated by others. Thus, while he may wish to speak his mind at any time, with all his customary hostility and vulgarity, he cannot simply say that he is free to do so because he has declined to play the role that has been designated for him.

If he is unwilling to provide the constructive model of behavior that millions of children need, then he should also be willing to forego some of the benefits of his status as a player, and be willing to recognize that he is part of the problem as well. In any event, he should refrain from being critical of a system that does not adequately provide role models and other opportunities for inner city youth, since he too is unwilling to make similar contributions. At the least, he should recognize that he *is* a role model whether he likes it or not and act accordingly. Similarly, during the play-offs last year, Shaquille O'Neal, another basketball star, was seen in an interview unable to spell the word "problem." He began to spell the word, stumbled, and then made a joke about it. He and the reporters broke out in raucous laughter, but this event did little to legitimize his status or to demystify any stereotypes about big, dumb, African American athletes. The message he sent was a symbolic one, but filled with dangerous implications for today's youth.

We hold athletes in high regard in this country, and whether we like it or not, they serve as role models. Instead of waiting for them to fall from grace, or to teach our children that it is acceptable to throw tantrums, to remain ignorant, or worse, that they will not be held accountable as long as they produce on the playing field, we should demand more from them. In a similar way, we should demand the same kind of accountability from teachers and other adults who serve as role models. This is an incredible responsibility, one that cannot be taken lightly or disregarded because it is inconvenient. If we do, we have become part of the problem and have no one else to blame when things go terribly wrong.

While I may not have had a positive role model early on, I think much of my early delinquent behavior can be explained through social learning theory and, by extension, the role models I did have. When I was removed from that environment and that group of individuals, however, I discovered two positive role models: Dan and Mary Ann. Although not necessarily through their object lessons as much as by observing their actions, I was able to modify my behavior and take on middle-class values. When I first told my wife the story of my past, she was shocked. She said that she would have never guessed that my background was anything other than middle class. To me, this only reinforces the point about the influence of mentors and role models.

To Foster Families

Since this played such an important role in my life, I would like to add a few words of advice or commentary to families who are considering taking in foster children, or those families who have already done so. Being awarded to the state and made a foster child is one of the most frightening things that could ever happen to a young person. More than likely, the child has ridden an emotional roller coaster for a long time, and this is the latest stop on a ride he or she would rather have not gotten on in the first place. In short, most of the kids in foster care have a variety of emotional and psychological problems. They may not always be of a serious nature, such as those that require medication or institutionalization, but they are significant nonetheless.

This is especially true if they have been cycled through the system before and if the quality of their care has been less than acceptable. As a result, children in this situation can easily become cynical, suspicious, and even hostile towards people. And then they arrive at your door. Will they make your life difficult? Probably, but there is a lot that can be done to minimize these problems—the most important of which is to give them time to adjust. They are carrying a lot of emotional baggage, and as we have seen, the nature of foster care really tests the child's ability to cope with adversity. If they come from an aggressive environment, which is likely, expect they will rely on the most familiar ways to solve problems. This is learned behavior, however, and like all behavior, it can be changed.

The worst thing that can be done, however, is to give them any reason to mistrust their new family or to expect them to be grateful for their new surroundings. If they have spent any time in the system, they are going to think the family is trying to take advantage of them in some way. This is true even in "model" families. As I mentioned, although somehow I intuitively thought that things were going to be okay when I moved in with the Hartmanns, I still looked for that angle. I was still suspicious of why someone would want to help me for no reason.

Like me, I suspect that most foster children will "test the waters" so to speak, if only to see what the boundaries are, but also to try to glean the reason for the generosity. It will be frustrating, but if the family sincerely wants to help, they will give the child time to adapt. Remember, these children will not act like your children—they are different and need to be reassured that the exploitation has ended.

Recall the impact of Dan's initial comments to me: telling me I did not need to ask permission to eat something or to use the television, and that this new environment was going to be my home for as long as I wanted. And it was not rhetoric—it was simply a statement that reflected how he was going to treat me—and I never felt more relieved. This does not mean that structure is not important: rather, it means that imposing it quickly may only exacerbate the problem.

The second, and perhaps most difficult issue, is fairness. It sounds so simple, but foster children are tuned into the double standards that exist between the biological child and the foster one. In my case, the situation was extreme, but I think it is important for families to treat all the children equally. This is especially true if the family expects the foster child to meet behavioral standards set for all children in the home. In other words, if you want them to act in a similar way, you have to treat them in a similar fashion. This is a difficult thing for families to do, because there will always be a distinction—there is a line drawn between the two types of children. Whenever and wherever possible, however (and I cannot underscore this enough), the foster family must attempt to blur those lines. Otherwise, the foster child will always sense a double standard, feel he or she is being treated unfairly, and act accordingly.

To Foster Children

In all likelihood, you have been in and out of the system several times and have had people, some of whom you trusted, take advantage of you in some way. It probably feels as though you are at the point where you cannot trust anyone—and you do not. I have been exactly where you are, so I understand completely.

For now, you need that suspicious nature and cynical attitude to survive, but try not to shut *everyone* out. I will not argue that a lot of people have tried to take advantage of you. What I will argue however, is that not everyone will do that. There are people who really want to help you. They are fewer in number, but there are more than you think. I think it is okay to try and find ulterior motives in the people you meet: if they are not concerned about your best interest, you have simply protected yourself. And if they are, these people, who can literally save your life, will understand. So go ahead: check them out, test them, see if they are worthy of your trust—and then let them help you. This is the hardest part, but if you are anything like I was, they will not disappoint you because you expected nothing from them. But not letting them try is the worst thing you can do.

A few years ago, the State of Connecticut advertised the state lottery in an attempt to attract people to participate. Their slogan was, "You Can't Win if You Don't Play." The same is true in your situation—if you do not let anyone help you, your situation will not get any better. If you give them a chance, you may find yourself writing about it someday. Sure, it could be a problem, and some of you will convince yourselves that it is too risky to try it. But the trick is to find the right person. And if you do, they may start you thinking that you can have a "normal" life and be a kid. I was lucky and I was probably the most cynical and suspicious person in the world. I never got scammed and few people "got over" on me. But I never lost hope, nor did I lose faith in myself. And if things get really crazy and you need someone to talk to, I will always be available and will always listen to you.

Finally, some of you may be wondering about my intentions in writing this book—am I seeking to profit from my experiences. Others might think I am being foolish for opening myself up to strangers like this. In a way, both points of view are correct and both are inaccurate. To address the first issue, let me assure all of you that my intentions are pure. I do not intend to profit economically from this book. In fact, I plan to donate all the royalties to charitable foundations for children. And with regard to the second point, you may be right: I might just be a "chump" for doing this. I am willing to take that risk, however, if it helps one of you.

If I profit in any way, it will be if someone reads this account, draws strength from it, and increases her or his resolve to continue their struggle. My goal then is simply to help other people who must witness the same kinds of emotional trauma that I have experienced. No child should be subjected to this type of life, but the realities of the world dictate a different script. I would like to change a few lines in the dialogue and make it a little better for even one young person.

A Final Word

After reading these pages, some people might feel sorry for me. Do not. This is not the point and would have made my efforts to make a few points futile. I wrote this book so that it might benefit a number of people, not to elicit the sympathy of friends or strangers. I think that I have finally gotten to the point where I can speak candidly about a number of painful issues. It still hurts a little, but perhaps a few people will read these pages and use them to help other kids who may not have been as capable of dealing with the situation as I was. This book was also written for those who are planning a career in the "helping" professions, such as social workers, child advocates, and counselors of various sorts. Finally, it was to serve as a reminder to those who are already in these professions of the significant impact, both positive and negative, they are having on the lives of the children in their care. I felt that my caseworkers were more concerned about their workload than the consequences their actions were having on me.

I strongly believe that if a person is deciding on a career in the "helping" professions, he or she should choose carefully, because it comes with a responsibility and obligation to the child first and the worker's needs second. Let us not lose sight of that simple but critical fact.

References

Anderson, E. (1991). *Streetwise.* Chicago, IL: University of Chicago Press.

Anderson, E. (1991). Neighborhood effects on teenage pregnancy. In C. Jencks & P. Peterson (Eds.), *The urban underclass* (pp. 375-398). Washington, DC: The Brookings Institute.

Duneier, M. (1992). *Slim's table.* Chicago, IL: University of Chicago Press.

Greene, M. (1993). Chronic exposure to violence and poverty interventions that work for youth. *Crime and Delinquency, 39*(1), 106-24.

Jencks, C., & Peterson, P. (Eds.). (1991). *The urban underclass.* Washington, DC: The Brookings Institute.

Kozol, J. (1990). *Savage inequalities.* New York: Crown.

Kozol, J. (1985). *Illiterate America.* New York: Plume.

Mayer, S. E., & Jencks, C. (1989). Growing up in poor neighborhoods: How much does it matter? *Science, 17,* 1441-45.

Merton, R. K. (1968). *Social theory and social structure.* New York: The Free Press.

Segal, T. (July 20,1992). When Johnny's whole family can't read. *Business Week,* 68-9.

Smith, T. (1995). Resource center: Finding solutions for illiteracy. *Focus, 72*(2), 1-3

Sutherland, E. (1947). *Criminology.* Chicago: University of Chicago Press.

Williams, T., & Kornblum, W. (1985). *Growing up poor.* New York: Lexington Books.

Williams, T., & Kornblum, W. (1994). *The uptown kids.* New York: Putnam.

Wilson, W. J. (1987). *The truly disadvantaged.* Chicago: University of Chicago Press.

Afterword

On Christmas Eve, while visiting friends and family in Connecticut and Massachusetts, I received a phone call from Mark: Daryl had finally called. He had been missing for approximately seven years, and my friends and colleagues in law enforcement continued to look for him without success.

As he recalls it, Daryl had been driving a tractor trailer all across the country for a period of time. He enjoyed the freedom the job held and even became involved in a training program for new drivers. One night in California, one of his students lost control of the rig and crashed, killing him. Daryl sustained a serious head injury and remained in the hospital for several weeks. After being discharged from the hospital, Daryl began to make his way back to Florida. While still suffering the effects of his injuries, and with several stops along the way, including an encounter with the justice system, he met a woman who served in the military. He moved in with her and tried once more to repair his life. It did not last. The relationship ended, he was laid off from his job, and he became depressed and concerned about where he was going to live. This has always been a problem for Daryl, but for some reason, perhaps a result of the injuries, getting older, or simply the wearing effects of a chaotic life, he called Mark and then contacted me.

After spending some time talking to him, Mark and I realized that Daryl was without resources, and, perhaps for the first time, without hope. As of this writing, we are trying to help Daryl find a job in the Pensacola area, as well as helping him regain some direction in his life. In many ways, his is the most tragic of stories. While some of the problems he has experienced have been the result of poor judgment, lack of insight, or simply stubbornness, in many other cases, they have been due to factors beyond his control. He is like many other people in our society, in that once the problems began, they quickly multiplied and became cumulative. And while his sense of self-reliance and independence have been able to sustain him for many years, the problems are now overwhelming, in part because his ability to cope with them has lessened.

At any rate, he is back now and although I remain concerned for his well-being, I must confess to a sense of optimism. In many ways, I see this recent development as a turning point for Daryl. I think he has finally realized that there are people who care about him and are willing to help. Further, I think he recognizes that he cannot succeed on his own, at least not any longer. He now knows that he will not, as he described to Mark, freeze to death on the streets with no one who cares about him or help him. By his own admission, this has motivated him to keep trying and to become socially, emotionally, physically, and economically self-sufficient. The difference, of course, is that being self-sufficient does not mean alone.

Selected Bibliography

Alexander, K. L., Beckland, B. K., & Griffin, L. J. (1975). The Wisconsin model of socioeconomic achievement: A replication. *American Journal of Sociology, 81*, 324-342.

Anatasi, A. (1988). *Psychological testing* (6th ed.). New York: Macmillan.

Anderson, E. (1991). *Streetwise*. Chicago: University of Chicago Press.

Anderson, E. (1991). Neighborhood effects on teenage pregnancy. In C. Jencks & P. Peterson (Eds.), *The urban underclass* (pp. 375-398). Washington DC: The Brookings Institute.

Aponte, R. (1991). Urban Hispanic poverty: Disaggregations and explanations. *Social Problems, 38*(4), 516-528.

Becker, H. (Ed.). (1964). *The other side*. New York: The Free Press.

Becker, H. (Ed.). (1963). *Outsiders*. New York: The Free Press.

Bell, D. (1953). Crime as an American way of life. In M. E. Wolfgang, L. Savitz, & N. Johnston (Eds.), *The sociology of crime and delinquency* (pp. 213-225). New York: John Wiley and Sons.

Black, D. (1983). Crime as social control. *American Sociological Review, 48*, 34-45.

Blau, P. M., & Duncan, O. D. (1967). *The American occupational structure*. New York: John Wiley.

Campbell, A. (1990). Female gangs. In C. R. Huff (Ed.), *Gangs in America* (pp. 163-182). Newbury Park, CA: Sage.

Chin, K. (1990). Chinese gangs and extortion. In C. R. Huff (Ed.), *Gangs in America* (pp. 129-145). Newbury Park, CA: Sage.

Cloward, R., & Ohlin, L. (1960). *Delinquency and opportunity.* Glencoe, IL: The Free Press.

Cohen, A. K. (1955). *Delinquent boys: The culture of the gang.* New York: The Free Press.

Conrad, P., & Schneider, J. W. (1980). *Deviance and medicalization: From madness to sickness.* St. Louis, MO: C. V. Mosby.

Cummings, S. (1995). Anatomy of a wilding gang. In S. Cummings & D. J. Monti (Eds.). *Gangs: The origins and impact of contemporary youth gangs in the United States* (pp. 49-74). New York: SUNY Press.

Dennis, E. E., Gillmor, D. M., & Gray, D. L. (1978). *Justice Hugo Black and the First Amendment.* Ames, IA: Iowa State University Press.

Doomhoff, G. W. (1978). *Who really rules?* London: Transaction.

Douglas, W. O. (1981). *The court years: The autobiography of William O. Douglas.* New York: Vintage Books.

Douglas, W. O. (1974). *The early years: The autobiography of William O. Douglas. Go east young man.* New York: Dell.

Duneir, M. (1992). *Slim's table.* Chicago: University of Chicago Press.

Dworkin, A. G., & Dworkin, R. J. (Eds.). (1982). *The minority report: An introduction to racial, ethnic and gender relations.* New York: Holt, Rinehart, and Winston.

England, P. (1992). From status attainment to segregation and devaluation. *Contemporary Sociology, 21,* 643-647.

Erikson, K. (1966). *Wayward Puritans.* New York: Macmillan.

Fagan, J. (1993). The political economy of drug dealing among urban gangs. In R. C. Davis, A. Lurigio, & D. Rosenbaum (Eds.), *Drugs and community* (pp. 203-224). Chicago: University of Chicago Press.

Fagan, J., & Chin, K. (1991). Social processes of initiation into crack use and dealing. *Journal of Drug Issues, 21,* 313-343.

Fagan, J. (1990). Social processes of delinquency and drug use among urban gangs. In C. R. Huff (Ed.), *Gangs in America* (pp. 129-145). Newbury Park, CA: Sage.

Farley, J. E. (1995). *Majority-minority relations*. Englewood Cliffs, NJ: Prentice Hall.

Feagin, J. R., & Vera, H. (1995). *White racism*. New York: Routledge.

Feyerheim, W., Pope, C., & Lovell, R. (1993). *Gang prevention through targeted outreach*. Washington, DC: Office of Juvenile Justice and Delinquency Prevention.

Flanagan, W. B. (1995). *Urban sociology: Images and structures*. Needham Heights, MA: Allyn and Bacon.

Frazier, F. (1957). *Black bourgeoise: The rise of a new middle class*. New York: The Free Press.

Gans, H. J. (1993). *People, plans, and policies*. New York: Columbia University Press.

Garfinkel, H. (1956). Conditions of successful degradation ceremonies. *American Journal of Sociology, 61*, 420-424.

Gibbs, J. (1966). Conceptions of deviant behavior: The old and the new. *Pacific Sociological Review, 9*, 9-14.

Gilbert, D., & Kahl, J. A. (1987). *The new American class structure*. Chicago: The Dorsey Press.

Goffman, E. (1963). *Stigma: Notes on the management of a spoiled identity*. New York: Simon and Schuster.

Goffman, E. (1961). *Asylums: Essays on the social situation of mental patients and other inmates*. New York: Anchor.

Gove, W. (Ed.). (1975). *The labeling of deviance*. New York: John Wiley.

Graduate Employee and Student Organization. (1995). *History of relations between graduate students and the Yale administration*. New Haven, CT: Author.

Gusfield, J. (1966). *Symbolic crusade: Status, politics, and the American temperance movement*. Chicago: University of Illinois Press.

Hagedorn, J. (1988). *People and folks: Gangs, crime and the underclass in a rustbelt city*. Chicago: Lakeview Press.

Hayward, M. D., Grady, W. R., & Billy, J. O. G. (1992). The influence of socioeconomic status on adolescent pregnancy. *Social Science Quarterly, 73*(4), 750-772.

Horowitz, R. (1983). *Honor and the American dream: Culture and identity in a Chicano community.* New Brunswick, NJ: Rutgers University Press.

Hout, M., & Morgan, W. R. (1975). Race and sex variations in the causes of the expected attainments of high school seniors. *American Journal of Sociology, 81,* 364-394.

Huff, C. R. (1989). Gangs, organized crime, and drug-related violence in Ohio. In *Understanding the enemy: An informational overview of substance abuse in Ohio.* Columbus, OH: Governor's Office of Criminal Justice Services.

Huff, C. R. (Ed.). (1990). *Gangs in America.* Newbury Park, CA: Sage.

Jankowski, M. (1991). *Islands in the street: Gangs and American urban society.* Berkeley, CA: University of California Press.

Jaret, C. (1995). *Contemporary racial and ethnic relations.* New York: Harper Collins.

Jencks, C. (1992). *Rethinking social policy: Race, poverty, and the underclass.* Cambridge, MA: Harvard University Press.

Jencks, C., & Peterson, P. E. (1991). *The urban underclass.* Washington, DC: Brookings Institute.

Jencks, C., & Peterson, P. E. (1979). *Who gets ahead: The determinants of the effect of family and schooling in America.* New York: Basic Books.

Jiobu, R. M. (1990). *Ethnicity and inequality.* New York: SUNY Press.

Joe, D., & Robinson, N. (1980). Chinatown's immigrant gangs. *Criminology, 18,* 337-345.

Joe, K. (1994). Myths and realities of Asian gangs on the west coast. *Humanity and Society, 18*(2), 3-18.

Katz, J. (1989). *Seductions of crime.* New York: Basic Books.

Kenney, D. K., & Finckenauer, J. O. (1995). *Organized crime in America.* Belmont, CA: Wadsworth.

Kitsuse, J. (1962). Societal reaction to deviance: Problems of theory and method. *Social Problems, 9,* 247-256.

Klein, M., Maxson, C., & Miller, J. (1995). *The modern gang reader.* Los Angeles: Roxbury.

Klein, M., Maxson, C., & Miller, J. (1989). Street gang violence. In N. A. Weiner & M. E. Wolfgang (Eds.), *Violent crime, violent criminals* (pp. 198-234). Newbury Park, CA: Sage.

Kluger, R. (1975). *Simple justice*. New York: Vintage.

Kozol, J. (1991). *Savage inequalities*. New York: Crown.

Kozol, J. (1985). *Illiterate America*. New York: Plume.

Krymkowski, D. H. (1991). The process of status attainment in Poland, the U.S., and West Germany. *American Sociological Review, 56*, 46-59.

Lemert, E. (1951). *Social pathology*. New York: McGraw-Hill.

Levin, J., & Levin, W. (1982). *The functions of discrimination and prejudice*. New York: Harper and Row.

Lewis, O. (1966). *La Vida: A Puerto Rican family in the culture of poverty*. New York: Random House.

Maas, P. (1973). *Serpico*. New York: Viking.

Makielski, S. J. (1973). *Beleagured minorities*. San Francisco: W. H. Freeman.

Mankoff, M. (1971). Societal reaction and career deviance: A critical analysis. *Sociological Quarterly, 12*(2), 204-217.

Marger, M. N. (1994). *Race and ethnic relations* (3rd ed.). Belmont, CA: Wadsworth.

Massey, D. S., & Denton, N. A. (1993). *American apartheid*. Cambridge, MA: Harvard University Press.

Maxson, C., & Klein, M. (1990). Street gang violence: Twice as great or half as great. In C. R. Huff (Ed.), *Gangs in America* (pp. 71-102). Newbury Park, CA: Sage.

Maxson, C., & Klein, M. (1989). Street gang violence. In N. A. Weiner & M. E. Wolfgang (Eds.), *Violent crime, violent criminals* (pp. 198-234). Newbury Park, CA: Sage.

Mayer, S. E., & Jencks, C. (1989). Growing up in poor neighborhoods: How much does it matter? *Science 23*, 1441-1445.

Mead, G. H. (1928). The psychology of punitive justice. *American Journal of Sociology, 23*, 577-602.

Mendelson, W. (1961). *Justices Black and Frankfurter: Conflict in the court*. Chicago: University of Chicago Press.

Miller, W. (1990). Why the United States has failed to solve its youth gang problem. In C. R. Huff (Ed.), *Gangs in America* (pp. 263-287). Newbury Park, CA: Sage.

Miller, W. (1975). *Violence by youth gangs and youth groups as a crime problem in major American cities.* Washington, DC: National Institute for Juvenile Justice and Delinquency Prevention, Office of Juvenile Justice and Delinquency Prevention, U. S. Department of Justice.

Miller, W. (1958). Lower class culture as a generating milieu of gang delinquency. *Journal of Social Issues, 14,* 5-19.

Moynihan, D. P. (1965). *The negro family: The case for national action.* Washington, DC: Office of Policy Planning and Research, U. S. Department of Labor.

Murphy, K. R., & Davidshofer, C. O. (1991). *Psychological testing* (2nd ed.). Englewood Cliffs, NJ: Prentice-Hall.

Murray, C. (1984). *Losing ground: American social policy 1950-1980.* New York: Basic Books.

Padilla, F. (1992). *The gang as an American enterprise.* New Brunswick, NJ: Rutgers University Press.

Parillo, V. N. (1980). *Strangers to these shores.* New York: Macmillan.

Powledge, F. (1970). *Model city.* New York: Simon and Schuster.

Ravitch, D. (1990). Multiculturalism: E pluribus plures. *The American Scholar, 59*(3).

Sagarin, E. (Ed.). (1971). *The other minorities.* Waltham, MA: Ginn.

Sanders, W. (1994). *Gangbangs and drive-bys: Grounded culture and juvenile gang violence.* New York: Aldine de Gruyter.

Santiago, A. M., & Wilder, M. G. (1991). Residential segregation and links to minority poverty: The case of Latinos in the United States. *Social Problems 38*(4), 492-515.

Schaefer, R. T. (1993). *Racial and ethnic groups.* New York: Harper Collins.

Schur, E. (1971). *Labeling deviant behavior: Its sociological implications.* New York: Harper Row.

Sewell, W. H., Haller, A. O., & Ohlendorf, G. W. (1970). The educational and early occupational attainment process: Replication and revisions. *American Sociological Review, 35,* 1014-1027.

Shaw, C. R. (1930). *The jack-roller: A delinquent boy's own story.* Chicago: University of Chicago Press.

Shaw, C. R., & McKay, H. D. (1942). *Juvenile delinquency and urban areas.* Chicago: University of Chicago Press.

Short, J. F., Jr. (1990). Cities, gangs, and delinquency. *Sociological Forum, 5,* 657-668.

Short, J. F., Jr., & Strodtbeck, F. (1965). *Group processes and gang delinquency.* Chicago: University of Chicago Press.

Sidel, R. (1986). *Women and children last.* New York: Penguin Books.

Smith, R. T. (1975). Societal reaction and physical disability: Contrasting perspectives. In W. Gove (Ed.), *The labeling of deviance* (pp. 147-156). New York: John Wiley and Sons.

Spergel, I. (1990). Youth gangs: Continuity and change. In N. Morris & M. Tonry (Eds.), *Crime and justice: An annual review of research,* Vol. 12. Chicago: University of Chicago Press.

Stone, J. (1985). *Racial conflict in contemporary society.* Cambridge, MA: Harvard University Press.

Steele, S., & Wilkins, R. (January/February 1993). Backtalk. *Mother Jones, 17,* 17-30.

Strickland, S. (Ed.). (1967). *Hugo Black and the Supreme Court.* New York: Bobbs Merrill.

Sutherland, E. (1947). *Criminology.* Chicago: University of Chicago Press.

Sutherland, E. (1937). *The professional thief.* Chicago: University of Chicago Press.

Swinton, D. H. (1990). Economic progress for black Americans in the post-civil rights era. In G. E. Thomas (Ed.), *U.S. race relations in the 1980s and 1990s* (pp. 345-371). New York: Hemisphere Publishing.

Sykes, G., & Matza, D. (1957). Techniques of neutralization: A theory of delinquency. *American Sociological Reveiw, 22,* 664-670.

Tagaki, P., & Platt, T. (1978). Behind the gilded ghetto. *Crime and Social Justice, 9*(2), 2-25.

Talbot, A. R. (1967). *The major's game.* New York: Harper and Row.

Tannenbaum, F. (1938). *Crime and the community.* New York: McGraw-Hill.

Thraser, F. M. (1927). *The gang: A study of 1,313 gangs in Chicago.* Chicago: University of Chicago Press.

Traub, S. H., & Little, C. B. (1985). *Theories of deviance*. Itasca, IL: F. E. Peacock Publishers.

U. S. Bureach of the Census. (1970). *Census of the population,* Vol. 1, Part 8: Connecticut. Washington, DC: Author.

U. S. Bureach of the Census. (1960). *Census of the population,* Vol. 1, Part 8: Connecticut. Washington, DC: Author.

U. S. Bureau of the Census. (1994). *Statistical abstract of the United States.* Washington, DC: Author.

U. S. Bureau of the Census. (1993). *Statistical abstract of the United States.* Washington, DC: Author.

U. S. Bureau of the Census. (1990). *Statistical abstract of the United States.* Washington, DC: Author.

U. S. General Accounting Office. (1989). *Nontraditional organized crime: Law enforcement officials' perspectives on five criminal groups.* Washington, DC: U.S. Government Printing Office.

Vigil, J. D., & Yun, S. C. (1990). Vietnamese youth gangs in southern California. In C. R. Huff (Ed.), *Gangs in America* (pp. 146-162). Newbury Park, CA: Sage.

Vigil, J. D. (1988). *Barrio gangs: Street life and identity in southern California.* Austin, TX: University of Texas Press.

White, G. E. (1982). *Earl Warren: A public life.* New York: Oxford Universtiy Press.

White, R. (1995). Race and poverty: An urban reality? In K. M. McNamara & R. McNamara (Eds.), *The urban landscape: Selected readings* (pp. 149-178). Landham, MD: University Press of America.

Wilson, W. J. (1987). *The truly disadvantaged.* Chicago: University of Chicago Press.

Wilson, W. J. (1978). *The declining significance of race.* Chicago: University of Chicago Press.

Wirth, L. (1945). The problem of minority groups. In P. I. Rose (Ed.), *Nation of nations: The ethnic experience and the racial crisis* (pp. 215-282). New York: Random House.

Wolfgang, M., & Ferracutti, F. (1967). *The subculture of violence.* London: Tavistock.

Wooden, W. S. (1995). *Renegade kids, suburban outlaws*. Belmont, CA: Wadsworth.

Woodward, B., & Armstrong, S. (1979). *The brethren*. New York: Simon and Schuster.

Yablonsky, L. (1957). The gang as a near group. *Social Problems 7*, 108-117.

Zinn, M. B. (1989). Family, race, and poverty in the eighties. *Signs, 14*(4), 856-874.

About the Author

Robert P. McNamara, Ph.D., is Associate Professor of Sociology and Director of the Center for Social Research at Furman University. He is also Director of the Greenville Social Services Training Institute. Dr. McNamara is the author of several books, including *Perspectives on Contemporary Social Problems*; *Crossing the Line: Interracial Couples in the South,* with Maria Tempenis and Beth Walton; *Crime Displacement: The Other Side of Prevention*; *The Times Square Hustler: Male Prostitution in New York City*; *Sex, Scams and Street Life: The Sociology of New York City's Times Square; Police and Policing,* with Dr. Dennis Kenney; *The Urban Landscape: Selected Readings,* with Dr. Kristy McNamara; *Social Gerontology,* with Dr. David Redburn; and *Managing a Deviant Status: Field Research and the Labeling Perspective,* with Deanna Ramey and Linda Henry. Dr. McNamara has also written numerous articles on a variety of topics and has been a consultant for state, federal, and private agencies on such topics as AIDS, drug abuse, urban redevelopment, homelessness, policing, gangs, and health care. He is currently working as a consultant for the Police Executive Research Forum and providing technical assistance training to police departments around the country on the problem-oriented policing model.

193